Roses and Rust

To Marianne, Erin, Maggie and Emma . . .
all of whom have taught me more about what is important than I ever seem to appreciate—*David*

For Jenny, Katherine and Laura Anne . . .
who have always been there, even when I could not be—*Robert*

Roses and Rust

*Redefining the essence
of leadership in a new age*

David Clancy and Robert Webber

Business & Professional Publishing

First published 1995
by Business & Professional Publishing Pty Ltd
Level 7, 10 Help Street, Chatswood, Sydney NSW 2067 Australia
Phone: (02) 415 1548 Fax: (02) 419 2948

© David Clancy and Robert Webber 1995

ISBN 1 875680 23 3

All rights reserved. Apart from any fair dealing for the purposes of study,
research or review, as permitted under Australian copyright law, no part
of this book may be reproduced by any means without the written permission
of the publisher.

The National Library of Australia
Cataloguing-in-Publication entry

Clancy, David, 1951-.
   Roses and Rust: redefining the essence of leadership in
a new age.

   Bibliography.
   Includes index.
   ISBN 1 875680 23 3

   1. Leadership. 2. Organizational change - Management.
I. Webber, Robert, 1953-. II. Title.

658.4092

Cover design by Drawing A Living

Printed in Australia by Ligare Pty Ltd

Contents

Preface   vii
Acknowledgments   viii
About the authors   ix
Introduction   xi

1. Seeing   1
2. Organisations   13
3. Transformation   39
4. Meaning   60
5. Directions   73
6. Connections   91
7. Knowing   108
8. Deciding   128
9. Helping   139
10. Energy   163

Appendix: Leadership   175
Endnotes   191
Bibliography   198
Index   201

*The Critical Leader must combine the
knowledge of systems thinking, the skill of the orchestral
conductor, the love of the gardener and the
wit of the hunted animal.*

Preface

The transformation of organisations to become adaptive and thereby survive and grow will only occur through increased understanding of the meaning of leadership. This understanding clarifies the concept of connections within organisations.

Part of the role of leaders is the linking of connections. This may be thought of as finding all the pieces of the puzzle.

The transformation of organisations also demands a rekindled care of the people within organisations, appreciating all the complexity and emotions of people.

For us, this means understanding the organisation to be a garden with every plant being nurtured so that the garden's beauty shows through. *Roses and Rust* explores the emerging themes of leadership and organisational transformation. These themes are emerging because process re-engineering has not delivered the adaptive organisation capable of growth through continuous change.

We have attempted to 'fit' pieces of the puzzle together through incorporating wherever possible the work of others in the field. It is our hope to begin to make the links with all the 'gardens' currently being nurtured so that we may all benefit.

We hope that we have added value.

Robert Webber
David Clancy

Acknowledgments

There are many people who have contributed to this book, both directly and indirectly. There are also many who have believed and trusted in the unfolding work.

We would like to thank in particular:

Marianne Kennedy
Jenny Webber
John Evans
Richard Pyvis
Barry Posner
Brian Carroll
Members of the Westpac Commercial Banking Learning Resource Centre
The Leadership and Management Development team, trainers and facilitators of the ANZ Bank
The Westpac Banking Corporation
The Globecon Group
Robert Lewers
Vince Johnson, Maurie Carr and Peter Buckham
Rod Ruthven
Helen Voogt-Dillon
The people of the Reptile Gulch group of companies
Jenny Gough and the people of SMB
Sue Woodward and the inaugural college curriculum people of TAFE
Ruth Matheson and Kate Eberle of Business & Professional Publishing for their faith, insights and support

and many, many others who have contributed to our learning over the years, especially when you thought that we were teaching you.

About the authors

Roses and Rust is the result of a Vital Connection between two people who came from different worlds to join forces to develop Critical Leaders in organisations. The 'home towns' of David and Robert are very far apart. David was born in Manhattan, New York, and Robert in Oakey, a very small country town in Queensland.

They started working together through a passion for using words like people, respect, decency and joy in the company of people who have been brought up to munch on different fare—productivity, performance indicators, marketing strategy, workplace units and rationalisation.

Major career and sight transformation came to David's life as he created his PhD dissertation on bank restructures during a hectic 1992–93 period. At the time he was Managing Director—Asia Pacific area of the Globecon Group Ltd. As he travelled the world talking to bankers, David examined how leadership and transformation were handled in organisations. With 12 years of 'real banking' behind him, David's conversations with his seminar participants led him to believe that leadership and transformation in organisations needed to be handled in radically different ways for the future. Consequently, David now works in cultural development for Westpac Banking Corporation in Sydney, Australia.

David's favourite quote about where the world of organisations is heading is attributed to the American baseball hero, Yogi Berra, who commented that 'The future ain't what it used to be.'

David is married with three daughters—whose lives have been forever transformed by his sight.

Robert's spirit drove him to run a bookshop, build a double-storey mud-brick house, read children's fiction and crime novels to a point of expertise, work as an educator, facilitator and teacher, and conduct his own business consulting to some of Australia's largest organisations. Mixed

About the authors

with a passion for music, family and New Orleans is a certainty that belonging to communities and 'nurturing the garden' lies at the heart of excellence and performance.

Robert is married, with two children who will always be more important to him than they will ever know.

David and Robert have established the Affiliates for Critical Leadership. The contact details are:

Affiliates for Critical Leadership
Glen Rae
Nadi Lane
Maleny Qld 4552
AUSTRALIA

David and Robert's hope is to make transformation a welcome word in organisations and to create leaders where once there were only managers—to help create places where their children will be happy to work.

Introduction

Two propositions:

1. Our organisations are like machines of varying complexity that can be assembled and reassembled in various structures to achieve particular ends—their success will depend a lot on getting their shape right. The organisation is like a great big meccano set which allows constant tinkering.
2. Our organisations have life—they are capable of growing and adapting depending on how their people are nurtured. The organisation is like a garden which demands care.

If you hold—and are not ready to be shaken from—the first of these propositions, this book is not your type of book.

Management and organisations are deep in crisis. Management has ceased to have the answers, and for more and more organisations this crisis is terminal. Organisations and their managers are searching for answers—they have tinkered with existing structures and paradigms, and they have failed to find the solutions. Current evidence says we have failed miserably in our attempts to re-engineer the organisation.

Studies of re-engineering say that company-wide change programs have failed to deliver what they promised. Now, before organisations work out how they are going to make money, they have to determine how they are going to survive.

We are on the brink of a new epoch for organisations, an epoch that will change the way that we live and work. Despite knowing that this new epoch is upon us, most organisations have no idea about how to ensure their own survival. Many organisations are unsure as to whether even their industry can survive, let alone specific organisations.

Introduction

Adapt or die

Our organisations are not responding effectively to socio-economic and technological changes manifesting themselves as unpredictable and threatening quakes—a defining feature of the age of discontinuity. Existing management practices contribute to the severity of their impact on the organisation and its people.

The failure of organisations to respond to these quakes is a result of our failure to perceive and understand the true nature of organisations. This failure is evident in the number of organisations that collapse or are brought to the brink of collapse; the cycle of restructuring and redesign of workplaces that invariably fails to improve productivity; the decline in the quality of working life and the increase in the amount of time spent at work.

Implicit in the management of most organisations today is the assumption that lies behind the first proposition—organisations are machines of varying complexity, which can be described and understood by organisational charts, inventories, instruction manuals and distribution points. Furthermore, 'proposition one' assumes that the organisation has a number of resources at hand, including its people, which can be added to or discarded, and it has a 'right' or 'best fit' structure for any given time.

Believing an organisation is a machine, a meccano set, provides so many barriers to performance that it is little wonder that so many organisations fail or reel from one painful episode to another. What is it that you think of when you think of a machine, or a meccano set? Do you think of pieces to be assembled, taken apart, reassembled; pieces that get bent and may get hammered back into shape. It does not talk back. It breaks and we replace it.

Ideas are left to the assembler of the machine. It rusts. The pieces (the people) are a resource to be replaced, discarded or built up at will, fed in as the machine demands. The shape never varies. It is utilitarian. It is not pleasing to the eye.

There is:

Introduction

No life.
No love.
No growth.
No inspiration.
No beauty.
No point.

Except for productivity. Productivity is the only point.

There is another way of understanding organisations. This alternative view of the organisation contains within it the conviction that change is inevitable and desirable for survival, and that tapping into the energies of the organisation is more important than getting the 'right' shape. It recognises the organisation as a self-organising adaptive system.

This is not merely a product of New Age thinking—the evidence is in. Kotter and Heskett have reported on the extraordinary results of organisations that build upon their people.[*] Science is also teaching us that organisations share all the characteristics of adaptive systems and, as such, treating the organisation as an organism is the only sustainable path for the future. It is not a 'nice to have'; it is not a luxury. It is *the fundamental and mandatory requirement for continued survival*.

Management continues its obstinate refusal to further its development. Organisations are moving too fast to listen. Managers do not hear how to cope with change. They are still buying ready-made solutions, but these have failed. Still they clutch at more and more straws—quality, self-managed work teams, re-engineering, cost-cutting . . .

The guarantees of success and survival have been removed. The lessons of the 'excellent' organisations of 1984 aren't worth noting today. In more than one organisation up to 70 per cent of the people are looking for a handout to help them leave. Senior executives are either not aware, unwilling to do anything or they simply do not know what to do about it.

---

[*] John P. Kotter and James L. Heskett reported in *Corporate Culture and Performance* that organisations that emphasised their people and leadership outperformed 'by a huge margin' organisations that focused on shareholders, customers and management. Over 11 years, sales were more than four times better and share prices were over 12 times higher.

Introduction

Organisations have three choices:

- management
- passivity
- leadership.

Of the three choices we believe that it is better to do *absolutely nothing* than to attempt to *manage* a system, which by definition is self-organising. Stop the feeble attempts at managing the people within organisations as if they were parts of a machine, as if we could ignore their complexity, as if they were pigeons or rats that could be controlled. Stop pretending that our very humanness need not be considered within the design of our work. We have permitted outside 'experts' and amateur behaviourists to infiltrate our workplace and let them alter the lives of the people who work there.

We have lost the confidence to run our organisations and we have lost the backbone to tell these 'experts' who fix nothing to leave. People cannot be treated as parts of a machine. They are the true wonder of organisations. The true power of organisations is the communities within them. The true disappointment of organisations is the treatment of their people—as though they did not feel. We manage the machine and:

- families are broken
- mothers return home, their self-worth lost
- fathers return home, their dignity driven out
- young people reject the idea of involvement or feel increasingly alienated
- we have no purpose
- all efforts are made for the shareholders (and they still don't succeed)
- we are driven by productivity (and we are no more productive)
- the organisation changes
- no one is secure
- we are told that we are not the right people
- many give up or die.

Introduction

The pace of the struggle to survive accelerates. Survival is the goal but it is increasingly clear that the common conception of organisations is not viable. People in organisations want to give up. These are people who have spent the last five years covering for the failings of management. Survival is only possible now by rallying the people of the organisation. One desperately hopes that this is accomplished before they finally stop caring.

Organisations in the past have defined the reason for their existence by their products or services. The imperative today for organisations is to transform themselves and to define their existence by the value they add to the lives of their people, their customers and to the marketplace.

The overarching imperative for managers is to embrace the metamorphosis from command and control to *Critical Leadership* (see Figure I.1). Leadership, by any definition, is essential in assisting organisations to transform themselves.

Critical Leadership provides organisations with the capability to define the meaning of work as:

- helping organisations to adapt and grow
- helping individuals to be the best they can be.

Critical Leadership demands a new understanding of organisations. It demands that we improve the performance of our organisations by using that understanding to tap into the energies that exist in every organisation. The Critical Leader has reconceived the organisation. Critical Leaders know that *people are the organisation*. Critical Leaders move with the *Vital Connections*.

Vital Connections begin with people. Ordinary people within the organisation know what is best, what is needed most. The establishment of the Vital Connections enlists energies within the organisation that have long been ignored or suppressed. Work changes. Work gets done, despite management failings; despite management's focus on process and training and technology; despite management's lapse of care for the living, breathing souls who are the organisation.

Introduction

Figure I.1: The Critical Leadership model

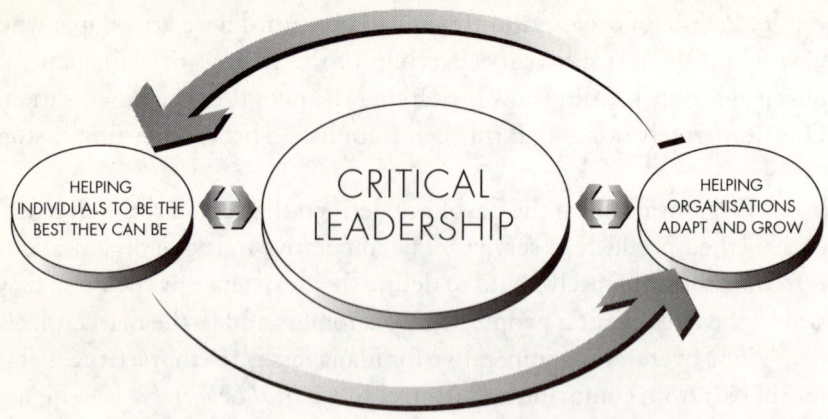

A Vital Connection can be:

... people who can and want to act directly to speed the transformation of the organisation from a soulless machine to a garden full of life. It might also be an idea, a process or approach that may or may not have immediately apparent or obvious application. Some of the connections within an organisation are surprising, and some of them are difficult to see right away.

The application of Vital Connections means:

- 'working underground' as long as possible—changing processes and systems and drawing attention to the changes after the event
- shifting from rules and regulations to relationships—with both customers and colleagues.

Locating and responding to the Vital Connections within your organisation is the difference between managing and leading. While a manager tries to control the system and focus on the particular, the Critical Leader will encourage both the growth of relationships and a focus on moving towards a preferred future.

Critical Leadership enhances the most Vital Connection of them all—the relationship between people and their work. In so doing, it does more than create the conditions for improved performance. It creates the foundation for organisations to work better, more simply and without the constant struggling that currently besets them. Critical Leaders are able to help establish harmony within the organisation because they give work a purpose, and allow people to apply their desires, thoughts and actions to the preferred future they have all determined for the organisation. The Critical Leader's reconception of the organisation involves:

Seeing: We must stop the way we currently see the shape of organisations, how they work and the purpose of their people. It is impossible to build organisations that will survive and prosper unless we change the way we perceive them. Using our present perception of them as complex machines we are not capable of moving forward. In the past we have only paid lip service to the idea of moving outside our comfort zones—to see anew is threatening and uncomfortable but necessary and exciting.

Organisations: Are they what we conceive them to be? Are they to be hammered into shape, new parts welded on when needed, or stripped off when we are done with them? What is their purpose? How does a leader relate to the organisation? When we see them differently the opportunities for them to adapt and grow become clear.

Transformation: In the past, organisational change happened in discrete bursts, in mini-revolutions. That kind of change is an outmoded concept. It said that we were one thing yesterday and today we have a new order—forget the past, it doesn't matter. But the past means everything to people. It is what enables organisations to move to the future—the experience and expectations of an organisation's people are built upon the past. We need to *transform* organisations to continuously adapt to the future without disenfranchising our people. This ability to engage everyone in continuous adaptation enables growth. Stop changing—transform, adapt, grow and reach for new potential futures.

Meaning: Kouzes and Posner, Covey and many other writers and thinkers have for years trumpeted the call for true leadership. Leadership is not about theories, offices, salaries and pecking order. It is about taking the responsibility for helping everyone in the organisation to achieve their maximum potential—for themselves, and for the organisation.

Unless the people can have a role in helping their organisation to adapt and grow, and unless their work also provides them with opportunities to achieve and connect in a personally meaningful way, there will be no organisation.

Directions: Once the people in the organisation are rediscovered they will willingly show all the consultants and management gurus how to get to the top of the highest mountain. Critical Leadership is about helping to find the maps and the compasses.

Connections: Everyday management of many organisations tells us all to focus on the details. The world of organisations is comprised of countless millions of people all 'doing the details'. They haven't a clue as to how their organisation connects together. Often those things in the organisation that should be simplest are shrouded in bureaucratic mystery. The truly complex web of people and relationships is ignored. Ask yourself: 'How many people in our organisation understand exactly how we make money?' Ask: 'What does it mean to work here?'

Knowing: The search for proof and 'reality' must be stopped. What we know is a result of how we have learned to see. Our present ways of observing, measuring and knowing fail to reveal the connections between everything and limit our ability to realise the multiple potential futures that are available to us. We have to unlearn much of what we already know before we can appreciate the complexities and possibilities of our organisations.

Deciding: Why is it when the subject of decision-making is brought up, the discussion focuses on power and status? Decision-making is about giving everyone the room to do the job that they need to do for the organisation to function efficiently. They know how to do this better than anyone else.

Helping: Life in an organisation is no longer about working there for 30 years to achieve the dubious honour of telling others what to do, or being told to leave. Leadership must be about building prosperous communities that provide some measure of security and a lot of dignity and respect, all the while asking 'How can I help?'

Energy: No organisation can act with integrity if it doesn't have mutually agreed values that are exhibited daily by its leaders. Every organisation's ethical approach must be directed equally at its shareholders, its people and its customers—each of them should be offered respect, dignity and acknowledgment.

The Critical Leadership–Vital Connections approach is to find the vibrant energy of the organisation and to work with it, helping it expand. This energy is expressed in the connections between people and customers, in the way work is conducted and the way the future is considered.

Old-style management will not be able to bridge the gap that separates the present from the future. Organisations that rely upon managers for their future will not make it. Those organisations that foster and nurture Critical Leadership throughout the organisation will.

Introduction

Roses and Rust explores all of these aspects of leadership within organisations. It provides a guide to examine how your organisation looks at and approaches work. It looks at all of the Vital Connections mentioned above and hopes to reveal some of the less obvious links between people and their working environment. It challenges you to think about whether your organisation is one of the few which will survive the transformation towards adaptivity and growth.

1.
Seeing

... an organisation is the entire set of relationships it has with itself and its stakeholders. An organisation is not a physical 'thing' per se but a series of social and institutional relationships between a wide series of parties. As these relationships change over time, the organisation itself changes. It becomes a different company. The failure to grasp this has prevented many an organisation from seeing that it is not the same because its environment, that is, its external stakeholders, has changed even though it internally looks the same. Since we are dealing with a system, a change in any one part potentially affects all other parts and the whole system itself.

Ian I. Mitroff and Harold A. Linstone[1]

We need to look at our organisations differently.

Organisations are governed by an archaic system of management that has outlived its use-by date. Although management has been able to guide organisations to prosperity in times of stability, it is unable to steer organisations towards sustainability for a future evolving chaotically and at lightning speed.

This is because management is based upon the notion that organisations are like complex machines—like a Swiss precision timepiece. Internal movement can be predicted, monitored and regulated. Its components can be improved or replaced. The clock needs winding and occasional maintenance. If something goes wrong it can be repaired. It is both a thing of itself and a sum of all its parts. Its organisation comes from an engineer or architect determining the order of things and thereafter looking after it.

Organisations are not like this at all. The perception of the organisation as a machine or physical entity is a death warrant for organisations. We need to alter our perceptions before we can begin to work with people to undertake the process of transformation now required for success.

We have to change our way of seeing; we have to change the way we 'know' our organisations and their people. The urgency of this change cannot be underestimated. The endless rounds of restructuring, conducted in a fruitless effort to get it 'right', are leaving the organisations that survive reeling. People are tired and hurt, and they have been promised no end to the pain. They wait for their turn to be asked to leave, because they do not know what they need to do to gain work security.

And all this has been for little practical benefit. The evidence is in—re-engineering and restructuring have not delivered the advantages they promised. We can only be sure that they are contributing to demoralised workplaces and organisations that are unsure of their future.

The need to look at our organisations differently has emerged for some of us out of a need to stop the pain and to end the uncertainty about the future, or it has come, for others, out of the knowledge that only through a different way of being can our organisations reach their full potential.

In this book we are inviting you to look at organisations as living systems that are defined by a complex set of internal and external relationships and connections of ideas. These include the forces that develop people's commitment towards working towards a preferred and sustainable future. We call these Vital Connections.

Many thinkers and management practitioners have urged the caretakers of organisations to recognise that an organisation is a network of relationships, or a system, rather than a machine. Mitroff and Linstone wrote that the failure to understand this can lead to managers making decisions based upon an inadequate understanding of the nature of their business.[2]

Seeing

Organisations are even more complex than this picture of them suggests. This does not make their governance more difficult; rather, by proposing a new way of looking at our organisations, this book provides an appropriate way of leading them to sustainable futures.

It is time for people within organisations to look beyond what they know, or think they know about organisations, and learn from other systems. Before we do this, we must know something about how we see. When we look at our organisations what do we see?

Oliver Sacks shares an invaluable story with us about a 50-year-old man, Virgil, who regained his sight after being blind for 45 years. What Virgil *knew* as a blind person he did not know when he regained his sight:

As we settled down, Virgil's cat and dog bounded in to greet and check us—and Virgil, we noted, had some difficulty telling us which was which. This comic and embarrassing problem had persisted since he returned home from surgery; both animals, as it happened, were black and white, and he kept confusing them—to their annoyance—until he could touch them too. Sometimes, Amy (his wife) said, she would see him examining the cat carefully, looking at its head, its ears, its paws, its tail, and touching each part gently as he did so. I observed this myself the next day—Virgil feeling and looking at Tibbles with extraordinary intentness, correlating the cat.[3]

We recognise what we see by the way our brains connect new information with prior knowledge. Virgil had no mental picture of a whole cat or dog; he only knew them by the parts that he could touch. On regaining his sight he had to try to correlate the whole.

Just as Virgil's paradigm of a cat or dog was a result of the way he had perceived them through touch, so too has our paradigm of organisations been influenced by centuries of industrialisation. We cannot help but see our organisations in terms of the division of labour, specialised tasks, structures of command and control, and linear work processes. It has been estimated by some scientists that 80 per cent of what we see is the result of prior information stored in our brains. Virgil had to *learn* to see his animals when he regained his sight. We have to learn to see and recognise our organisations as being complex sets of ideas and relationships that are inextricably linked to their environment.

We have to unlearn the mechanistic, or machine, model and replace it with a morphogenetic[*] view of organisations, which allows us to see them as systems of energy sharing some of the basic properties of matter—rhythm and movement. Although their webs of living thought and actions may not always be visible, we have to learn to nurture them, work with them, in order to achieve the organisational transformation that is becoming imperative.

Like all living systems, the organisation's patterns of rhythm and movement are rarely predictable, but their order is revealed over time. Successful organisations generate energy from within and they are capable of spontaneous growth and transformation. Organisations, like life forms, can grow from a seed to plant, and it is hard to explain why some seeds prosper and others fail.

This way of seeing our organisations must extend to *in*sight as well as outer vision. Internal connections are as essential to the organisation as the external connections with the environment. Experts hired to 'fix' a 'broken' organisation will never know it or understand its problems as well as its own people do. Critical Leaders come from within an organisation, although they may seek help from people with expertise to help them with the transformation.

Self-organising adaptive systems

The organisation is a self-organising and adaptive system; it shares the properties of other living systems. Unlike 'physical' or mechanical systems such as computer circuits, plumbing, wiring or heating, organisations and

---

[*] *Morph*: form; *genesis*: coming into being.

Seeing

other living systems constantly change within themselves as a result of stimulation from their environment.

These systems—organisation, ecosystem, ant colony, family—are in a state of constant change. The human body, so often described as a machine, is anything but a machine. It completely renews 98 per cent of all its cells each year. The body can be described, as other systems can, as a self-organising system that is in a constant state of movement and flux.[4]

Self-organising adaptive systems are also able to generate an internal response to information they receive. Oliver Sacks writes that we need:

... a new view of the brain, a sense of it not as programmed and static, but rather as dynamic and active, a supremely efficient adaptive system geared for the needs of the organism—its need, above all, to construct a coherent self and world, whether defects or disorders of brain function befall it. That the brain is minutely differentiated is clear: there are hundreds of tiny areas crucial for every aspect of perception and behaviour ... The miracle is how they all co-operate, are integrated together, in the creation of a self.[5]

The potential for organisations to create a coherent 'self and world' is not recognised by managers who regard their organisations as programmable machines. Instead of providing the organisation with the support necessary for all its component parts to co-operate in response to a turbulent world, they give their machine a new appellation and expect that it will then be different. When managers nominate that the organisation will have a 'quality culture', or a 'customer driven culture' or a 'sales culture', or whatever, they destroy the opportunity for the organisation to grow and acknowledge its sense of self or identity. The Critical Leader discovers, reveals and nourishes the sense of uniqueness of culture that is the essence of every organisation.

Sacks invites us to consider that a new definition of 'health' may be the ability of the organism:

... to create a new organisation and order, one that fits its altered disposition and needs, rather than in the terms of a rigidly defined norm.[6]

If we look at our organisations in this light, a lot of them are not healthy, whatever their current financials may look like. A sound financial statement may only indicate a temporary strength, not health. Most organisations currently try to adapt and create a new order by altering bits of the machine without regard to the adverse consequences this has on the strength of the relationships that enable it to function. Managers have generally failed to recognise that it is these relationships that help the organisation to create new order.

The ability of a system, any living system, to prosper on the strength of its internal relationships is recognised more by scientists than it is by the people who govern our businesses. Brian Goodwin, a professor of biology, invites us to 'consider the ant and be wise':

Ants and other social insects such as termites and bees present us with a paradox that is good for proverbs. The activity patterns of individuals often appear to be very disorganised, and by any of the normal criteria they cannot be described as intelligent. No one has succeeded in teaching individual ants anything; for instance, they are simply incapable of learning to discriminate one direction from another in finding a food source . . . However, put a bunch of ants together and what marvels of collective activity result! Individual neurones are not very intelligent either, but a lot of them hooked up together can result in remarkably interesting and unexpected behaviour.[7]

The ability of ants and termites to build colonies is a result of the connections the insects make with each other—they are stimulated by the activity of others. Alone, they will remain inactive or their behaviour will be chaotic.

The transition from chaotic movement in isolated individuals or low density colonies, to rhythmic behaviour in a colony, occurs when the density reaches a critical value. The group behaves in a collective mode that could not be predicted from the behaviour of individuals.[8]

| Seeing |

The success of organisations depends upon the strength and energy in their inner and outer connections. Seeing, recognising and knowing the interconnectiveness of all the relationships and energies that act in a constantly shifting array of patterns holds the only future for organisations.

The interconnectiveness has always been there. Organisations have always been self-organising and adaptive systems. As we built industries, our way of looking at the world changed and we lost sight of the interconnectiveness of things. Like Virgil regaining his sight, we have to learn to see again.

The key qualities of self-organising adaptive systems are listed in Table 1.1.

Table 1.1 The qualities of self-organising adaptive systems

Defined by relationships
Capable of adaptation and learning
Individuality, linked to a universal (e.g. Fido, Spot: dogs; Westpac, Citibank: banks)
Require information from their environment
In motion, continuous change
Complex

Syzygy

The nature of organisations has changed over the course of this century, and if they are to succeed in the future, another revolution as fundamental as the transition to the industrial era is required. This time, however, it will not be a transition over time; it must be sharp, disjunctive, far-reaching. It must redefine every aspect of the way we work and relate to each other through our work. The companies that do not transform themselves in this way will not survive.

There are three dimensions of organisations that can be examined running through this century and into the new era for organisations—governance, people and structure.

The beginning of this century saw the transfer of responsibility for the operations of the business from owners to managers. The day-to-day operation of the business became far too complex and time-consuming for the owners, and new skills were required to keep organisations on track.

The people, the workers, 'progressed' from being regarded as 'hands' to being subordinates ('less than ordinary') and employees (from the French *employer* 'to use').

The structure of organisations went from being linear (owner—hands) to the organisational structure we all know, of hierarchical authoritarianism, strict division of labour, chains of command, control and reporting; an organisational structure that suffocates creativity and innovation, debasing the crucial role of people and their Vital Connections.

The manager has only been effective in adaptive systems when a great deal of regulation and control extends into the organisation's environment. The role of managers in these times has been overvalued—organisations have the capacity to be self-organising. There is a hidden truth in the belief that the best work, and the most valuable work, gets done when the boss is away.

Organisations don't work, or they fail to achieve their potential, because watchmakers, accountants and engineers have been put in charge of 'gardens'. They try to control and limit something that should not be controlled. Of course they can achieve some success. A plant can be treated as a self-contained mechanism. It can be distorted and made to grow into a certain shape. It can even be impressive in this form, but it will never be an integral part of any natural environment. It will never know its ultimate potential or true form.

The business world is not a controllable world. The best that can be achieved is that an organisation develops the syzygy that will enable it to make decisions and develop actions to carry it into a preferred future, rather than the one it will have if it continues on its present path.

| Seeing |

Syzygy is defined in the *Macquarie Dictionary* as:

... the conjunction or opposition of two heavenly bodies; a point in the orbit of a body, as the moon, at which it is in conjunction with or in opposition to the sun.

Syzygy is a time of enormous forces and energies. Organisational syzygy offers the opportunity to align the three dimensions of governance, the people and the structure, in order to generate powerful actions and energies within an organisation.

It requires that we see and understand these three dimensions within a new framework, as a part of being able to see and know the organisation from a new perspective.

An organisation's people can no longer be regarded merely as arms and legs implementing the commands of inaccessible decision-makers further up in the hierarchy. People come to work because they have aspirations for success in collaboration with other people—a collaboration that is denied to them without organisations. They have been identified within a few organisations as the 'intellectual capital' of the business. This book explores their role in the organisation's web of ideas and relationships that give it an identity and place in the world. These are the Vital Connections. They are 'vital' to both the success of the organisation's adaptation and growth, and to its people finding a high and worthy purpose to their work.

The era of the manager has passed, although too many organisations don't know this yet. It is time to enter the era of the leader.

This book is about the Critical Leader who works with Vital Connections. This is the person who is able to achieve syzygy in the organisation. Critical Leadership is also a means of addressing the need for work to provide a compelling meaning that adds worth to the lives of those connected to an organisation, particularly its employees and their customers.

Critical Leadership is not the province of a few. It is necessary that all people within the organisation embrace its values and focus.

As we enter, at warp speed, a new era for doing business, organisations do not have the luxury of taking an evolutionary path towards their future. The path towards the future is to work with the energies and forces that are within each organisation, to build the syzygy that provides organisations with their 'health', their ability to be continuously able to adapt in order to flourish in the world of living systems. Syzygy can only occur when there is Critical Leadership *and* intellectual capital *and* the organisation is regarded as a continuously adaptive system, as illustrated in Figure 1.1. Any other combination will have forces working against each other.

Figure 1.1 Syzygy and ways of seeing the organisation

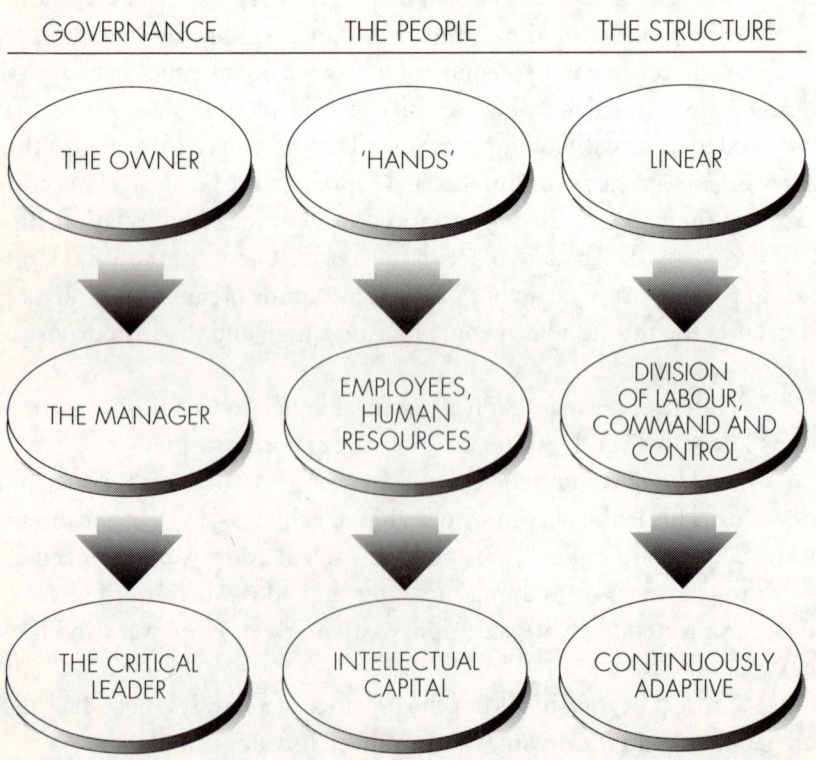

| Seeing |

We invite people to read *Roses and Rust* and to become Critical Leaders in their own organisations. The nature of the organisation is determined by how it is perceived. If the people within organisations perceive that they are inextricably a part of a web of other living systems, capable of continuously adapting its internal order and form, the nature of work will radically change and the opportunities for harmony within work become possible again. This is the promise of Critical Leadership and syzygy.

There is no known better path and there are no half measures. The organisation is either treated as a self-organising adaptive system like a garden that thrives and prospers, or it is regarded as a machine that will rust and die. 'Management' can no longer bring life to organisations.*

---

* It has been the authors' practice to promote the discussion of ideas through disseminating books in organisations. In one organisation, with 300 staff and one site, we gave a copy of Ricardo Semler's *Maverick* to the top three managers. One manager returned it unopened—a casual perusal of the cover was all that was required to convince him that it was too radical for him. Another manager thought that it was full of good ideas, but not for this particular organisation. The third thought it had the right ideas for the organisation but he had no idea how to make things change. These three managers focused on the operation of the machine.

We gave a copy of the book to a leader in another organisation that employed thousands of people in more than 100 sites throughout the nation. This leader came back and said, 'This is do-able.' Over the next 12 months, job titles were scrapped, responsibilities were spread throughout all levels of the organisation and people's energies were harnessed. People started to appreciate the power of an adaptive organisation and sales grew.

Discovery

At the conclusion of each chapter, where appropriate, you will find a continuum of ideas drawn from the chapter. The aim is to assist you to see things differently, discover the position your organisation holds on the continuum and to determine appropriate directions for transformation.

Seeing

The machine	*The garden*
The organisation is a machine	The organisaton is a self-organising adaptive system
Managers control the organisation	Leaders help develop organisational syzygy
People are the organisation's most valuable resource	People find a high and worthy purpose to their work
The way to the future is an evolutionary path	The path to the future is to work with the organisation's energies and forces

2. Organisations

The distinguishing manifestations of life are: growth through metabolism, reproduction, and the power of adaptation to the environment through changes originating internally.

Macquarie Dictionary

What is it that makes a garden a compelling image of the organisation of the future? It is alive. It is full of spontaneous diversity. Without this diversity it becomes formal, uncomfortable and stilted. It requires a level of continuous care that cannot always be predicted. In a garden, there are only probable outcomes. It flourishes. It adapts to harsh winters and grows again each spring. It changes continuously. It requires a lot more work than the machine. It is the love of the gardener which brings and maintains life. The relationship between the gardener and the garden determines each season's outcome. Both garden and gardener respond to their environment.

Pictures of the future

The decision on how to view organisations is yours. The 'organisation as a machine' image will ensure a continual round of futile re-engineering, which in turn will have a variety of unpleasant consequences.

- Customers will lose their connections to the organisation time and time again. Every time a customer loses a connection, the service link is made weaker and there is one less reason for a customer to remain loyal. The present practice of frequent restructures means that organisations are building on a customer foundation of sand.
- The financial soundness of the organisation will suffer. While organisations look for the 'best structure', they are forever knocking something down and rebuilding. This process, which was originally done in the guise of cost cutting, is now an enormously wasteful and expensive exercise.
- People within organisations will be undervalued. In the re-engineering process they are often treated as parts or resources, rather than as a Vital Connection with the customer and within the organisation. People become expendable. If the machine doesn't perform better, they will lose their jobs; if the machine does perform better, they may also lose their jobs.

People are tired, people are hurt. Those who remain after a re-engineering exercise have the low energy and outlook of survivors. We have gone from 'Thank God it's Friday' to 'Thank God I've got a job' when, if the organisation is to flourish, we need to inspire a 'Thank God it's Monday!'[1]

Energy, mind, soul

As our understanding of science becomes more complex, so the body of evidence to suggest that organisations share the characteristics of living organisms grows. Margaret Wheatley, in her book *Leadership and the New Science*, considers the fields of energy that govern life.[2] Her case is that while machines strive for equilibrium, a state of rest where all forces are balanced (a net result of zero), organisms are held together by connecting forces as they engage with the environment, grow and evolve.

For an organisation, these forces are people who contribute waves of energy when they make external and internal connections. We have all

| Organisations |

experienced, as Wheatley has, organisations that feel alive and have energy, where others feel dead and unresponsive to their environment (customers). An organisation's culture, its picture of the future, values and work practices are either aligned, with connecting forces pulling everyone to the future, or they are conflicting forces that confound and confuse the people who work there.

An organisation has a 'mind' or intellectual force behind it—just as organisms do. Like organisms, every organisation has to process the information it gathers about its environment. The capacity to transform this information into knowledge is increasingly important. The value of an organisation's intellectual capital escapes those who treat it as a machine. They send people with knowledge and wisdom out the door in exchange for a short-term reprieve on a balance sheet.

There is a case for the soul of the organisation too. Just as values, convictions, preferences, loyalties and beliefs are a part of a person's life, they are also a part of an organisation. We 'know' our organisation's beliefs about its people, its customers and its suppliers. People find meaning in life beyond what is scientifically proven. People need to find meaning in their work, too—to be able to put 'heart and soul' into one's work is one of our most desired goals.

Whether the organisation is viewed as a machine or a living organism makes a fundamental difference to the way it is managed and the decisions that are made about its future, its people and the way it connects with its customers. The perception of the organisation makes a world of difference to whether the organisation fails or prospers in the quakes that are to come.

The strength of connections

Organisations prosper and grow on the strength of their internal and external connections. Organisations that look after these connections increase their own potential for survival. Those leaders who treat the organisation as a balance sheet, with people being shifted from the asset to

Table 2.1 Organisation: machine or garden?

The machine Focus on:	*The garden* Focus on:
Management	Critical Leadership
Product or service delivery	A quest for meaningful work
Productivity as management practices	Productivity as the liberation of people
Tool kit to fix problems	Nurturing as care
Provable 'truth'	Many potential futures
Fixed image of the organisation	Adaptive, growing, fast and flexible
Blame and avoiding failure	Learning from experience, including 'failure'
Left brain focus	Whole brain focus
Control all variables	Adaptive to shifting variables
People held to processes and tasks	People own the whole system
Numerous reports	A few reports on the things that matter
Outside 'experts' redesign system	Outsiders help the whole system to make improvements
Managers intervene at times of panic	Leaders provide continuous care

| Organisations |

The machine
Focus on:

People are expendable costs

Fear of uncertainty

Critical mass

The garden
Focus on:

People are intellectual capital

Trust in the future

Vital Connections

the liability side of the ledger and back again, have failed to understand that people *are* their business—it is people who bring energy and life to the internal and external connections of any organisation.

Each time an organisation is restructured or re-engineered, each time a leader fails to take the opportunity to make people feel valued, each time processes and rules take precedence over a customer, the external connections and the forces that hold the organisation together are loosened. People, out of loyalty to their connections, their colleagues and their customers, have brought organisations back from the brink. They will not do this forever. If the forces that hold the people—who are the organisation—together continue to be loosened, the 'centre will not hold'.

The single most important matter that leaders of organisations must address is the provision of meaning for work. The way you view your organisation and the way you manage your people determines what working there means. Table 2.1 illustrates the opposing aspects of the organisation as a machine or as a garden. The remainder of this chapter explores each of these opposing aspects.

Management and Critical Leadership

Management is concerned with predictability and order. It is concerned with command and control of the organisation. Rules that have been established on the basis of past experience direct actions. Management, although designed to keep the machine working efficiently, is the rust of the organisation. It is the aspect of the machine which has lost its ability to shine any longer. No amount of polishing enables rusted metal to support the stress of functioning. Replace the machine, but the rust will reappear and the machine will need to be replaced yet again.

In contrast to management, leadership is concerned with producing change to achieve results. While there have always been successful leaders in business, they have often been the heroic individual or the entrepreneur. Sometimes they have done the right thing, and sometimes they have led the organisation and its people over the precipice.

Leaders are the gardeners of the organisation. The question which must be asked here is 'Does this gardener love their garden?' Critical Leadership provides a meaning for the role. Critical Leadership is defined as:

- helping organisations to adapt and grow
- helping individuals to be the best they can be.

Critical Leaders, at all levels of the organisation, are crucial to the success of the organisation and its people. They provide the Vital Connection between the two.

Decisions and actions made by Critical Leaders are considered in the light of whether they contribute to the organisation's ability to grow and adapt or whether they help people to be the best they can be. It is important that Critical Leaders find a way of expressing the need to develop a workplace based upon dignity, respect and kindness.

Business is beleaguered by consultancies and academic institutions offering leadership development programs. However, little, if anything, changes after someone participates in a leadership course. Any consideration of leadership will fail to lead to the development of new behaviours if it does not address the role of leadership in cultivating purpose in the organisation.

As Peter Drucker writes:

Organisations

Leadership is not by itself good or desirable. Leadership is a means. Leadership to what end is thus the crucial question.[3]

'Management' is a liability to any business today. Its focus on order, control and predictability fails to develop within organisations the energy of its people and within its connections a responsiveness to the environment. It is common to find managers acting as part of the corporate immune system, inhibiting the growth of leadership, particularly within their people.

The role of managers and Critical Leaders within organisations is fundamentally different and these differences are illustrated in Table 2.2.

Table 2.2 Managers and Critical Leaders

Managers	*Critical Leaders*
Organise and make 'controllable' things happen	Help the organisation to adapt and grow; help people to be the best they can be
Define maximum specifications	Define 'minimum critical specifications'[4]
Determine processes and rules to be followed, and tell people how to do their work	Negotiate boundaries and ask questions
Exert authority and control through organisational hierarchy	Exert authority and influence through Vital Connections

Facilitating adaptation and growth

Within each business there must be people who look after the functions of planning, budgeting, organising and monitoring. However, while we have a surfeit of managers within our businesses we do not have enough Critical Leaders.[*]

Critical Leadership is about involvement with people—but not the control of people. Instead, Critical Leaders uncover the Vital Connections between the people of the organisation and the organisation itself. Helping people to achieve their best goes beyond merely being effective in their job. It goes beyond bridging the gaps in skills—the difference between the person's current ability and what the job requires—to enabling people to bring their full gifts, talents, interests and dreams to work.

Many companies are now making explicit the need for dignity and respect at work through codes of conduct and similar statements. That they feel the need for this is a validation of the idea that companies have been concerned with *things and processes* rather than *people* for too long. There is no doubt that the business world lost sight of its people, despite clear messages about the need for dignity, respect and community in the workplace. Now, from all fronts, the case for a moral and spiritual reform of the workplace is being championed.[**] (The ethical dimensions of Critical Leadership are discussed in Chapter 10.)

Defining 'minimum critical specifications'

Job descriptions and instruction manuals that delineate every minute aspect of the job must be replaced by everyone doing 'what has to be done'.

---

[*] The reader is referred to (1995) *Enterprising Nation: Renewing Australia's Managers to Meet the Challenge of the Asia–Pacific Century*, Report of the Industry Task Force on Leadership and Management Skills, AGPS, April. This is also known as the Karpin Report.

[**] The case has some strong proponents: M. Scott Peck argues the case for 'civility' in *A World Waiting to be Born: Civility Rediscovered*; Alfie Kohn, in *Punished by Rewards*, presents the evidence against manipulative practices of rewards and incentives at work; Peter Block, in *Stewardship*, presents the case for choosing 'service' over self-interest.

Any attempt to define all of the job—the maximum specifications—ultimately fails as work and customer expectations become more complex and less predictable.

When leaders establish the *minimum critical specifications* of a job they are stating the 'must do's' simply and clearly—the rest of the job is up to the people who do it.

For example, Revco, a major US retailer, replaced customer service training by prescribing three simple specifications as a good minimum for customer service. Employees must:

- greet every customer every time he or she enters the store
- ask every customer if he or she needs assistance every time they see the customer searching for a product
- make eye contact with every customer every time they speak to him or her.

Outcomes of this measure included the elimination of a lot of wasted effort, service staff who knew the minimum that was expected of them, a 90 per cent compliance with the specifications, a decrease in customer service complaints and an increase in comments from satisfied customers.[5]

Negotiating boundaries and asking questions

The people who do the job, know best how to do the job. This assertion threatens the core assumptions of management. Instead of management following its traditional path of controlling what happens, Critical Leaders negotiate the boundaries and then support the people who make things happen.

When managers define both the maximum specifications of the job and the processes and rules to be followed, they remove people's ownership of their work, restricting their desire and ability to respond to customers. Negotiating boundaries includes mutually determining the limits to employees' authority and the extent to which people need to involve others, including the leader.

For this to be effective, there should be free access to all information. Information is now power, more than it ever has been. Critical Leaders ensure that *everyone has free access to whatever information they decide they want*. This is the opposite of the pervasive military notion that people should receive information only on a 'need to know' basis.

The need for maximum specifications and most policies, rules and procedures are the result of individual and organisational traumas. They are put into place after a mistake or failure—to stop it happening again. They can prevent people from doing the job that needs to be done. Leaders face a difficult task when they try to take the attention of people away from the rules and manuals. It is best done quickly. One company turned its performance around by getting people to work together:

We burned 21 inches thick of policy manuals. We eliminated reports and signoffs. We installed trust.[6]

Critical Leaders spend time with their people asking questions about business and what should be done. (This is discussed in Chapter 5.) They do not need to tell people what to do. Instead they create an environment that enables people to make their own contributions to the workplace.

Exerting influence through Vital Connections

The chain of command and control that exists in organisational hierarchies is no longer appropriate.

How many of us have worked in the same building as our CEO and the top team and never seen them? One of us worked for a senior manager who, on his way to his office, walked past 20 staff in the department and then spent his week talking only to the three or four people who reported directly to him. Every survey we have done of workplace satisfaction has recorded people asking for managers to stop and talk to them.

Leaders need to work with their Vital Connections in order to exert authority and influence. These Vital Connections may or may not have authority in their own right. They will certainly listen and be prepared to follow new paths.

The quest for meaningful work

At best, the machine organisation achieves improvements in the development and delivery of its products or services. At worst, it remains static, in which case it will finally be destroyed by competition or other forces, and is a dehumanising place to work. Employees are rarely asked 'What does it mean to work here?' And if they are, the culture is often such that a truthful answer will not be received if a manager is asking.

In their work on the need for a new strategy to take organisations into the future, Hamel and Prahalad wrote:

The responsibility of an employee to work diligently for the success of the firm, the cornerstone of the contract of employment, has a counterpart. It is senior management's responsibility to imbue work with a higher purpose.[7]

Even the assurance that 'people are our greatest asset' merely affirms the view of the organisation as a machine. Only when people are given the freedom to 'achieve and connect' at work does work have meaning. People must have the opportunity to identify avenues to grow within the work that they do.

The garden organisation recognises and builds upon the fact that people care about their work and seek opportunities at work to grow and learn. As noted by Alfie Kohn after his extensive research on workplace motivation:

Motivation is typically highest when the job offers an opportunity to learn new skills, to experience some variation in tasks, and to acquire and demonstrate competence.[8]

Productivity and liberation

Machines may operate with one person or a small group of people taking responsibility for their success but, in the garden, the leader's contribution to success is to prepare the environment for everyone to flourish and contribute. The operators of machines direct their energies to removing operational variables. The caretakers of the garden direct their energies on the life forces of the garden's inhabitants. Individual forces are freed and allowed to combine.

From Jack Welch, CEO of General Electric:

We can say without hesitation that almost every single good thing that has happened within this company over the past few years can be traced to the liberation of some individual, some team, or some business.[9]

Critical Leadership prepares the environment and becomes obsessed with gaining the voluntary involvement of people to the fullest possible extent—their hearts, minds and limbs. Critical Leadership encourages the development of a spirit of discovery and involvement, rather than the directive approach of training people in processes and their improvement. Allowing the people power to direct their jobs and to make contributions to the entire system is a sign that they are trusted and respected. Trust in the workplace makes work easier as people are open about what they can and cannot do and they seek ways of helping each other. People *are* the organisation, so we need to allow and encourage a diversity of feelings, emotions and thoughts. These should all be welcome aspects of the workplace.

Fixing and nurturing

For some reason managers have a need to find and fix people problems. Just as a work process can break down and need fixing, people can develop attitude problems and require remedial attention or corrective action. Organisations produce checklists for work processes and the management of people, such as performance appraisal forms and job descriptions. These are the equivalent of a mechanic's tool kit.

The purpose seems to be that if all items get a tick, or the people can be made to fit a performance curve, if the organisation's periodic maintenance is attended to, then the organisation can be diagnosed as making progress.

However, because people are the essence of the organisation, it is incongruous to approach them as though a simple oil change will keep them ticking. People are the organisation, so we need to allow and encourage a diversity of feelings, emotions and thoughts. These should all be welcome aspects of the workplace.

Provable truth or potential futures?

There is a best way to build a machine and there is a right way to operate it. An organisation, as a machine, has a 'best' structure to facilitate the command and control of all its functions. Managers try to set a course for the future that they may measure as three, five or even ten years hence.

The organisation seen as a garden has many potential futures and many possible forms. The aim is not to establish predictability, as it is for the machine. Instead, it is for order without predictability. Order is created in this organisation by the alignment of the forces—vision, culture, values, capabilities and work practices—that are capable of pulling it towards an uncertain but promising future.

Adaptive, growing, fast and flexible

For a machine to provide a new or different outcome, or to process material in a different way, it will require dismantling and reassembling. Often the same bits will be reassembled but in different places. Sometimes the only change that happens in response to the changing environment is a change in the management team—who they are, where they sit. The machine organisation responds slowly to changes in the marketplace or to innovation by trying to make the changes fit with its own structure.

This is in contrast to an organisation that is fluid and adaptive, where:

Expertise, tasks, teams, and projects emerge in response to a need. When the need changes so does the organisational structure.[10]

As noted above, the organisation seen as a garden has many potential futures and many possible forms. The aim is not to establish predictability, as it is for the machine. Instead, it is for order without predictability. Order is created in this organisation by the alignment of the forces—vision, culture, values, capabilities and work practices—that are capable of pulling it towards an uncertain but promising future. John Kotter and James Heskett researched the fortunes of more than 220 organisations over an 11 year period. The high performing organisations had cultures that anticipated and adapted to changes in the environment with:

. . . widespread enthusiasm, a spirit of doing whatever it takes to achieve organisational success. The members are receptive to change and innovation.[11]

This kind of organisation regards these kinds of changes as opportunities for transformation, rather than as calls for restructuring.

Learning from experience, even 'failure'

In the machine, when things go wrong there will certainly be blame and sometimes punishment. It is not unusual for the punishment to take the form of humiliation, such as an 'award' for worst performance.

In the garden, a 'mistake' is an opportunity to learn. Warren Bennis recalls a successful business leader who said, 'I try to make as many mistakes as quickly as I can in order to learn.'[12]

A whole brain focus

The way we think influences the way we see our organisations—what information we choose to receive and how we respond to that information. Business has come to respect the left brain focus on data, processes and proof—things that are ideal for the machine. Oliver Sacks draws our attention to the deficits of a left brain approach to life when he writes:

> *... it is the right hemisphere which controls the crucial powers of recognising reality which every living creature must have in order to survive. The left hemisphere, like a computer tacked onto the basic creatural brain, is designed for programs and sematics.*[13]

Ned Herrmann, writing of the 'costly rise of the left',[14] discusses how the path of industrialisation has favoured the development of production-oriented and business-centred behaviours. This typically sees the reward of orderly, replicable and fact-driven behaviours and the disapproval of spontaneity, risk-taking and intuitive behaviours. The machine requires evidence and ultimately proof that something will work.

In the past organisations have been able to observe changes and plan a response to them based upon evidence and experience. But in the age of discontinuity changes can happen so quickly that often there is no time to learn from others, even assuming that your organisation aims merely to follow the market leaders. Risks and decisions must be taken, and flexible and committed employees must be prepared to make those decisions work.

When there is no one right answer there is a need to consider each opportunity, risk, problem or plan from a 'whole brain' perspective. Questions such as the following need to be asked:

- What data do we have?
- What is the best way of organising ourselves for this?
- How will this affect our people?
- What are the long-term implications and possibilities?

Another 'whole brain' approach is to assemble teams to approach projects. A left brain assault team comprising only rational, logical and practical people is likely to miss new opportunities for the organisation and its people. Giving a planning role to the typically right brain training department will probably lead to wonderful but impossible plans. The garden grows through diversity, so *difference* must be publicly valued and sought out.

Max De Pree, CEO of Herman Miller (US), an organisation that achieves an extraordinary return to investors, wrote:

In addition to all of the ratios and goals and parameters and bottom lines, it is fundamental that leaders endorse a concept of persons. This begins with an understanding of people's gifts and talents and skills . . . Recognising diversity gives us the chance to provide meaning, fulfilment and purpose, and which are not to be related solely to private life any more than are such things as love, beauty and joy.[15]

Control or respect?

How many manuals or pages would it take to document all the written and unwritten policies, rules and regulations of your organisation? How frequently are these out of date? How many people are involved in rewriting these when the organisation must change or a part of it dies? Is it ever conceivable that the average employee would know most of these, why they exist and how they are used in the quest for greater productivity?

It is the legacy of bureaucratic or machine organisations to attempt to prescribe, in minute detail, every action and every conceivable

| Organisations |

situation. It is also the legacy of the machine organisation to maintain overbearing, costly layers of management to enforce and interpret the policy, rules and regulations. The results? Slow response times, inactivity and high costs.

It is the intent of the garden organisation that all the garden's inhabitants understand that 'everything will always be different'. It is the intent of the garden organisation to have only the bare minimum of policies, rules and regulations. This is so people can know and apply them. The garden is also about treating the people of organisations as responsible adults rather than as delinquent children, engaging them and empowering them, rather than simply controlling them. There is no longer a need for costly layers of management. The result? A reliable, responsive and cost-effective organisation.

Who owns the system?

A legacy of Taylorism is that jobs, like machines, have often been reduced to their most basic components or functions. The approach is very much a part of the 'left brain' approach to work—measuring outputs and processes, dividing jobs into small bits and allocating tasks.

In the largest machines it is common for managers not to be concerned about staff turnover, because the parts of each job are so simple that little training is required for someone to become proficient at their job. When people are promoted in the machine organisation they often continue to define themselves simply by the processes and systems under their control. They fail to coach, care for and empower their people. These organisations place great value on activity—*busyness*.

In the organisation that is alive to its environment, people are responsible for more than the routine tasks that make up their job. They are encouraged to look at and make decisions for the entire system. People at all levels understand the economics of the business, the technologies that affect it, and the needs and wishes of customers, colleagues and shareholders.

When people are promoted in this garden organisation, they leave their old work behind and allow other people to 'own' that work. There is a strong focus on the future and a lot of connections achieved through talking and action. A duty of care is assumed by the people of the organisation. Learning is valued—and learning can only occur when there is time for both reflection and action.

Measuring success

We once worked in an organisation that received a report on business activity every Wednesday at lunchtime. If the results were below budget (which was fairly often), the rest of the managers' week was spent analysing, interpreting and looking for culprits or problems in the system. There was no time for leadership.

We have also worked in an organisation that produced for its management team a monthly financial statement for the various arms of the organisation. At the end of an hour discussing them, without making plans for the future, copies of the statements were returned to the financial controller so that staff would not have access to the figures. The customer feedback sheets were never discussed and there was no concern expressed for how the staff felt about working there.

On measurement, Jack Welch's advice is:

Too often we measure everything and understand nothing. The three most important things you need to measure in a business are customer satisfaction, employee satisfaction, and cash flow. If you're growing customer satisfaction, your global market share is sure to grow, too. Employee satisfaction gets you productivity, quality, pride, and creativity. And cash flow is the pulse—the key vital sign of a company.[16]

Organisations

The nature of the measurements and the act of measuring can have adverse consequences for any organisation. When you walk into a garden you know if it is flourishing without having to consult a chart that records the measures for the growth of the plants. When you walk into a business, as Margaret Wheatley points out, you *know* whether it is healthy or not. Chapter 7 discusses the nature of measuring and knowing.

The pitfalls of expert advice

If you believe that an organisation is like a machine then it is also possible to think that outside 'experts' can come up with better designs for your machine. For many years we have watched organisations engage 'experts' to help them redesign organisational structure and work processes, without seeing any improvements in productivity. The proposition that outsiders can come up with a model for an organisation is based upon two fallacies:

- that the organisation is a structure that has a best shape
- that people will accept a model or changes that are imposed upon them.

Margaret Wheatley's eloquently presented argument that the organisation is not a machine strikes directly at the heart of the first of these fallacies. Each organisation's culture is unique to it because that culture is based upon internal connections, the connections that are forged by and rely solely upon human contacts.

The second fallacy is related to the first. Externally directed re-engineering breaks these existing connections and negates the contribution that the people within an organisation can make. Some consulting companies 'cheat' in this matter. They design changes to the total process and then hand it over to internal project teams and proclaim that the organisation 'owns' the project. There are two common outcomes that arise from this approach:

- the consultants blame the organisation or the project teams for not implementing their ideas correctly
- the project teams, drawn and withdrawn from the line, become or are regarded by their colleagues as elitist, and they cease to have a connection with the people that matter.

Either way, restructuring is failing left, right and centre. Hamel and Prahalad report on recent studies:

Restructuring seldom results in fundamental improvements in the business. At best it buys time. One study of 16 large US companies with at least three years of restructuring experience found that although restructuring did improve a firm's share price, the improvement was always temporary. Three years into restructuring, the share prices of the companies surveyed were, on average, lagging even further behind index growth rates than they had been when the restructuring began.[17]

The alternative? The alternative is to engage the right outsiders, who bring a commitment to the organisation, and energy and ideas rather than answers. They become a small part of the organisation's project team.

The outsiders are only one more element in the transformation process that sees 'expertise, tasks, teams and projects emerge' in response to the environment. They do not attempt to redesign the system, but help employees to make improvements to the existing system.

Providing continuous care

We worked with one manager who said that his people knew when they were doing a good job because then he would not come out of his office.

| Organisations |

Most large machine organisations work in much the same way—everything's fine until something goes wrong and then there are outside 'experts' everywhere, road shows and assurances that 'people really matter'. Then come the sackings.

These interventions are a waste of time. Organisations have to adapt and grow in volatile times. As Figure 2.1 shows, each organisation will reach a point of organisational and environmental uncertainty when it has to make decisions about the path for its future. It can apply a short- or long-term focus; it can use Critical Leadership to choose a path of renewal and growth, or it can look back on the successful practices from a past era and start an inevitable decline.

Figure 2.1 Organisational development

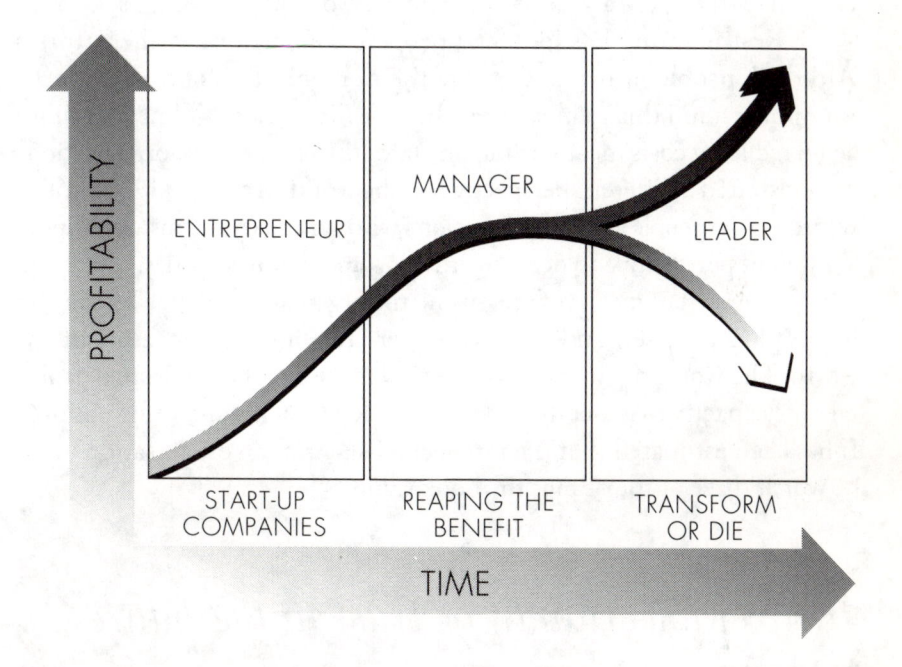

Source: Adapted from George Ainsworth-Land's (1986) *Grow or Die*, New York: Creative Education Foundation.

33.

Raising an organisation above the plateau, or reversing a decline, requires the spirit and commitment of renewal. It is necessary to call upon the energy and vision that starts new ventures to bring to an organisation new life.

From expendable costs to intellectual capital

In the Depression, the Matsushita company of Japan only required half of its workforce to make household appliances. Instead of laying off half of the labour force, management asked people to work half days in manufacturing. In the first half of the day they made equipment; during the second half, the employees went into the cities to sell. This generated an extra $US10 million a year in sales and everyone kept their jobs.

Restructuring has loosened people's connections to their work. Although people hear that they are their organisation's greatest asset, they understand this to mean that they are dispensable. Time and time again reducing costs means laying off staff. Just as a Japanese organisation demonstrated a different perspective on the workforce in the 1930s, truly regarding the people as the organisation's wisdom and consciousness brings a different perspective to decision-making and planning today.

The current means of measuring the organisation's value by counting its physical assets and costs no longer provides a true measure of its worth. The worth of an organisation now resides in its intellectual capital—its capacity to generate and use knowledge, skills and information. It has been estimated that the intellectual assets of an organisation may be worth three or four times the book value.[18]

Fear of uncertainty or trust in the future?

In the machine organisation, people know that their jobs are at stake. They also know that they are undervalued. They suspect that their

Organisations

organisation is not set up to cope with the quakes that will hit it in the near future.

In the garden organisation, people feel valued and able to participate in 'growing the business'. They see that if they can find meaning for their lives through work they will cease to fear the future. Future quakes will call upon their knowledge and resources in unexpected ways, but they have the confidence that they, as a team, have the ability to respond.

People have pulled many organisations through the first quakes—they will not do it again without the support and acknowledgment of their leaders. In machine organisations their contribution may not be fully recognised and appreciated, as managers may not understand the vital contribution their people made.

In garden organisations people are already preparing for future quakes.

Critical mass or Vital Connections?

Traditional wisdom has it that when a system or an organisation achieves a critical mass, change and progress is inevitable. When, for example, 30 per cent of an organisation has accepted a goal or undergone training, the organisation will perceptively shift and the momentum will gradually capture everyone.

This may have been true in times of stability. It may also hold true today for initiatives of limited scope such as product launches. However, leaders wishing to effect a transformation within their business no longer have the time to rely upon achieving a critical mass. Other change agents know full well that 'corporate immune systems' are activated as soon as the system is challenged from within. These can effectively kill off new initiatives before they have gathered any sort of momentum.

Very few of us work for transformational or visionary leaders. Trying to achieve a critical mass when 'management' is at work is virtually impossible. An understanding of the forces and energies operating within an organisation and the nature of Vital Connections provides the opportunity to evade the corporate immune system and to introduce transformation programs.

Ultimately, the machine model for an organisation has been the root cause of organisational failure. It prevents managers from encouraging the organisation to be adaptive to the environment. This will continue to be the case until managers change their understanding of what constitutes an organisation.

| Organisations |

Discovery

Organisations
Compare your perceptions of the organisation with those of other people.

The machine   *The garden*

Management	Critical Leadership
Product or service delivery	A quest for meaningful work
Productivity as management practices	Productivity as the liberation of people
Tool kit to fix problems	Nurturing as care
Provable 'truth'	Many potential futures
Fixed image of the organisation	Adaptive, growing, fast and flexible
Blame and avoiding failure	Learning from experience, including 'failure'
Left brain focus	Whole brain focus

Roses and Rust

The machine	The garden
Control all variables	Adaptive to shifting variables
People held to processes and tasks	People own the whole system
Numerous reports	A few reports on the things that matter
Outside 'experts' redesign system	Outsiders help the whole system to make improvements
Managers intervene at times of panic	Leaders provide continuous care
People are expendable costs	People are intellectual capital
Fear of uncertainty	Trust in the future
Critical mass	Vital Connections

3.
Transformation

Virtually everyone who joins an organisation . . . does so with two needs: to give something and to get something. Obviously we want to get something. Money and status, for instance, are among the 'motivators' for people seeking organisational employment . . . What is less obvious is how much—how almost desperately—we humans want to give as well as receive. Most of us have a profound need to be of service to the agencies for which we work, to be truly useful, even essential, in our jobs.

M. Scott Peck[1]

Our prevailing system of management has not only failed to meet the challenges of the changing environment, it has done considerable damage to organisations and their people. Consider for a moment the pain that the people in your organisation may have had to bear over the last few years. How would you judge their happiness at the moment? If your organisation is like many organisations, the people will be hurting or, at best, confused.

Management, by its very nature, will continue to hurt more and more people, because it fails to recognise the possibilities and nature of the organisation, and the role of people in its success. The transformation that organisations must undertake if they are to survive will not succeed unless the people become volunteers to the cause.

With its mechanistic view of organisations and its reliance on command and control, rules, policies and past practices, management is unable to respond with the imagination and innovative practices that are now required. Furthermore, it does not allow for, or promote, imagination and innovative practices within the organisation. Management's response to a challenge is to control the resources—to tinker with the machine. The people who were once a declared asset to the organisation suddenly find that they are a cost-centre, a liability, like other resources.

The capacity to transform the organisation is fundamental to any organisation's future. And this capacity is beyond the ken of management.

People involved in change programs are fond of quoting Einstein, who is attributed with saying: *'No problem can be solved from the same consciousness that created it.'*

Management has created most of the problems that beset organisations. Even those organisations that continue to enjoy the success offered by a competitive advantage due to product, service or market niche are still failing to maximise their potential if they are governed by our current paradigm of management.

Critical Leadership creates a perspective to help managers go beyond what they know and to open up new areas of action as leaders, including the continual transformation of an organisation. The template is based upon a different consciousness of an organisation—the self-organising adaptive system—a garden.

Critical Leadership also provides meaning for the workplace. Organisations are complex systems which rely upon the strength of their internal and external connections. The strength of these is an indicator of the degree of harmony both within the organisation and between the organisation and its environment.

The leaders of an organisation, and in this case we mean the formal leaders and not necessarily those that show leadership, have the most power and influence in determining the nature of the organisational culture. This culture determines how people relate to each other as colleagues and customers.* Until the advent of the quakes that continue to

---

*A few years ago the Melbourne *Age* referred to a merger of two major national companies as the perfect marriage of two companies that treated the customer with contempt. These cultures were certainly renowned.

shake organisations to their very foundation, the question of the nature of an organisational culture was largely of interest only to consultants and academics. It is now a matter of performance.

In 1992, John Kotter and James Heskett published a landmark study[2] that provided the heads of organisations with a choice. Would they rather:

- manage their business for a 682 per cent increase in revenue, or a 166 per cent increase
- improve the return to shareholders by 900 per cent or by 74 per cent
- expand their workforce by 282 per cent, or by 36 per cent
- be responsible for contributing to an increase of 756 per cent in net income, or 1 per cent?

Their research of the performance of 220 companies in 22 different industry groups over an 11 year period identified the highest performing companies, those that achieved on average the extraordinary results reported above, as having strategies that demonstrated a commitment to customers *and* shareholders *and* employees.

Kotter and Heskett also made the following damning indictment, based upon their research:

In most firms, managers do not care deeply about customers and shareholders and employees. They may value one of their constituency groups, or perhaps even two, but not all three. More likely, they have been taught to care more about their kind of work (accounting, engineering, etc.), their department, specific products, or only themselves. Nor do most managers believe in the importance of leadership at multiple levels in the firm.[3]

Managers are failing their people, their customers and their shareholders in their quest for the simple answer and the short-term result. The appalling legacy of management is that it has failed to understand the role of the organisation's people in achieving success. Caring 'deeply' about the employees is more than recognition schemes, pay-for-performance and the occasional 'Thank you'. Involve them in determining how the organisation can best grow and adapt, and help them to be the best that they can be.

The model of Critical Leadership enables people at multiple levels within organisations to achieve the transformation that will be required before the results reported above can be gained. Critical Leadership, with its dual focus on meeting the needs of the organisation and its people, provides the appropriate model for transforming the organisation so that it is able to respond to its environment. It will guide the leader to develop the interconnectedness between customers *and* staff *and* shareholders. It will also guide the development of the strategies that Kotter and Heskett found led to extraordinary performance.

Critical Leadership demonstrates a commitment to:

- the customer, by helping the organisation to adapt in response to its environment
- the shareholders, with its focus on helping the organisation to grow
- the people within the organisation, by creating an environment that helps them to be the best they can be.

The first Vital Connection

Effective organisational transformation begins with the people within the organisation. They are the first Vital Connection. In the organisation as a machine, managers frequently fail to recognise the importance of work needing to have 'meaning' or be purposeful. The need for work to have meaning, if it is recognised at all, is often translated into shareholder, service or product terms—return to shareholders, zero defects, customer satisfaction and so forth. None of these is completely satisfactory.

Despite the work by Hertzberg, Maslow, Lewin, McGregor and numerous others, and despite every piece of research that indicates that people want jobs that allow them to achieve and contribute at work, organisations continue to define people *only by their part in a process*.

Managers and leaders can create, in M. Scott Peck's terms, 'civil' or 'uncivil' workplaces. They can dangle carrots and sticks, or they can create an environment that promotes intrinsic motivation and people who 'pursue optimal challenges, display greater innovativeness, and tend to perform better under challenging circumstances'.[4]

Critical Leaders create a fulfilling workplace and one of their first achievements is the alignment of the energies within the organisation, taking people forward to a preferred future. They achieve syzygy between the organisation's governance, people and structure.

A 'preferred future' is not a projection of the present, not just more of the same. It is the future that everyone in the company desires for themselves and that anticipates the future needs of the customer and shareholders.

The alignment of energies goes much further than this as Critical Leaders define and explore the potential of all the Vital Connections that make up an organisation. Recognising and working with an organisation's Vital Connections distinguishes the leader who sees the life of an organisation from the manager who sees a machine. This alone creates a different meaning for the culture.

Imagine if the organisation were described, as it could be, in the terms Sir Charles Sherrington used to describe the brain:

The human brain is an enchanted loom where millions of flashing shuttles weave a dissolving pattern, always a meaningful pattern, though never an abiding one, a shifting harmony of patterns. It is as though the Milky Way entered upon some dance.[5]

Managers do not observe or use the dancing patterns of an organisation. There are within all organisations interconnections that are sometimes visible and sometimes invisible, running beneath the surface of things. Knowing that they are there creates meaning. Using them to help the organisation to adapt and grow and the people to become the best they can be is the proper purpose of leadership.

A powerful example of one of the more visible connections is the 'moment of truth'. Named and described by Jan Carlzon, CEO of Scandinavian Airlines System (SAS), an organisation that focuses its energies on this connection demonstrates an understanding of its interdependence with its environment:

Last year, each of our 10 million customers came in contact with approximately five SAS employees and this contact lasted an average of 15 seconds each time. Thus, SAS is 'created' in the minds of our customers 50 million times a year, 15 seconds at a time. These 50 million 'moments of truth' are the moments that will ultimately determine whether SAS will succeed or fail as a company. They are the moments when we must prove to our customers that SAS is their best alternative.[6]

Directing the energy of the people within SAS into a Vital Connection with the customer led to a transformation that we could call a quake. Within one year SAS went from a potential loss of $20 million to earn $54 million.

The impact of the moment of truth at SAS goes well beyond that company. Just as the flap of a butterfly's wings can cause storms on the other side of the world, Carlzon's sharing his understanding of this Vital Connection is contributing to organisational service initiatives around the world.

The Vital Connection with the customer also affects the flows of energy and power within organisations. Carlzon makes it very clear that contributing energy to the customer relationship does not take energy out of the organisation. Rather, it creates internal energies and strengthens the internal connections.

The organisation can only deliver on the moment of truth with the customer if everyone in the organisation has the ability to do whatever it takes to make it effective:

Transformation

Giving someone the freedom to take responsibility releases resources that would otherwise remain concealed . . . An individual without information cannot take responsibility; an individual who is given information cannot help but take responsibility.[7]

All of the Vital Connections within an organisation are linked. Increasing the energy that is fed into one relationship leads to an increase in the energy in another set of connections; weakening a Vital Connection will weaken all Vital Connections. Consider the impact of a success. Consider the impact of retrenchments. The meaning of work fundamentally changes as the energies of the Vital Connections change.

The Vital Connection with the customer creates such a powerful meaning of the nature of work that job descriptions and instruction manuals become redundant. Nordstrom's staff handbook contains all the guidance that people need to work there. It is a single 12 by 20 centimetre card that reads:

We're glad to have you with our Company.
Our number one goal is to provide **outstanding customer service.**
Set both your personal and professional goals high.
We have great confidence in your ability to achieve them.

Nordstrom Rules:
Rule # 1: *Use your good judgment in all situations.*
There are no additional rules.

Please feel free to ask your department manager, store manager or division general manager any question at any time.

There are many stories of Nordstrom's legendary service. A friend of ours came back from a visit to the US singing the store's praises. He and a colleague were shopping for a particular style of shoes. Unfortunately, they were out of stock at the time. The sales assistant apologised and ascertained that the Australians would be in the store for another hour. Within that hour, the assistant had left the store, obtained the shoes and found his customers. He apologised for the inconvenience and gave his customer a free pair of socks.

Defining work through the Vital Connection with the customer, and creating an environment that allows people to make a difference to the strength of this connection, recognises the need of people to be able to 'give' to their jobs. As Vital Connections are explored, the outdated realm of management and the machine is left behind.

A Critical Leader's job is to strengthen all the connections involved in the workplace and to bring syzygy to them. The Critical Leader looks beyond the external 'moment of truth', which creates a customer driven company, to developing an organisation that is truly and continually adaptive to its environment, and engages the commitment of its employees as well.

The Critical Leader helps people to be the best they can be. This only can be done if the leader cares for people and builds an environment where people can care for each other. Caring is not necessarily used in a soft or fuzzy sense. Any organisation needs people who can help it to adapt and grow. Furthermore, no organisation can afford to have people who do not share its values, goals and ethics or who, by their actions, are not contributing to gaining the preferred future. An organisation is not a family, but any organisation can offer to its people the membership of a community. All organisations are built upon connections and relationships. A true community is an organisation in a higher form. The nature of the community that a Critical Leader can strive for and develop using Vital Connections is best described by M. Scott Peck:

Specifically, for me, community requires communication—and not the mere exchange of words, but high-quality communication. The quality of group communication is so poor in our typical business and social organisations that I designate them as pseudocommunities or pretend communities. For

Transformation

the most part, keeping their interaction both light and polite, their members are only pretending to communicate. A genuine community, on the other hand, is a group whose members have made a commitment to communicate with one another on an ever more deep and authentic level. There are very few true communities.

When a group does make such a commitment . . . wonderful things will begin to happen. The members transcend their narcissism, coming not only to respect but to appreciate their differences. Long-buried resentments are surfaced and resolved. Enemies are reconciled. Hard eyes become soft, and swords become feathers.[8]

Such communities represent an adaptive organisation growing on the strength of its visible and invisible connections. Organisations that are based upon a true community foster leadership at all levels and titles become irrelevant. They also prepare the way for the organisation to become self-organising. The steps within mechanistic organisations towards teams and empowerment fail in time. They are used as a panacea when the machine is malfunctioning. In an organisation that is a garden the people form a Vital Connection with the future. Teams will succeed in this environment because empowerment is the way things are done—it is not there to be 'put in' or 'taken away'.

Organisations that are communities in a turbulent business world provide the opportunity for people to grow and connect, to be valued and to value others. True communities are so important that Peck urges that community building must take place *before* an organisation makes decisions. Organisations suffer daily from the effects of decisions that are made in the absence of a true community. Commitment is a part of belonging to a community. Many of these decisions may be minor and cause little more than an irritant, but they remain a symptom of an underlying malaise. Decisions without commitment to a community are far more destructive and costly in their impact. In 1994, executives of the ANZ Bank and union negotiators reached an enterprise agreement. The much publicised agreement amounted to nothing when it was rejected by the bank's staff.

Critical Leaders can use Vital Connections to transform an organisation to respond better to its customers and to better meet the needs of its people, or they may go further and develop a truly adaptive community. (The former may not be the latter—the latter will certainly be the former.)

An acknowledgment of the power of Vital Connections makes much of 'management' redundant. Management needs command, control and order. It fears what it cannot control or predict. Vital Connections are flows of energy that are often invisible. When science told us of chaos in nature, it also opened the door for us to appreciate and use the apparent disorder within our organisations.

Nature and organisations share chaos—an inability to predict what will happen next. But chaos is not just about being unable to predict events and outcomes. As described in *The Quark and the Jaguar*, it is also about the major impact that small variations can have on a system:

. . . there remains the widespread phenomenon of chaos, in which the outcome of a dynamical process is so sensitive to initial conditions that a minuscule change in the beginning of the process results in a large difference at the end.[9]

Over time, chaos theory has shown us that every system has an inherent orderliness—'strange attractors' will ensure that a system never goes beyond certain boundaries.

When the random behaviour of unpredictable systems is mapped on a computer it is discovered that their random behaviour never exceeds certain finite boundaries. These boundaries are known as 'strange attractors' and enable chaos to be further defined as 'order without predictability'.[10]

The organisation's strange attractors are, we suspect, people's desires to *achieve* and *connect*. We believe that Rabbi Kushner was the first to describe achievement and connection as two driving forces within people. (Their description as strange attractors is our own and is, of course, open to challenge.)

These two desires define the boundaries of our endeavours. Work is valued if it provides people with the opportunity to achieve and connect. Connection is a part of Vital Connections and includes relationships with work, home and family, spirituality and play.

Management's controls are not needed because the behaviour of all people at work is bound by the common needs as expressed by these strange attractors. Critical Leadership focuses on valuing these attractors and providing people with opportunities to achieve and connect.

Approaching transformation

Critical Leaders use Vital Connections to drive transformation. They have greater success in overcoming the resistance offered by either the corporate immune systems or by inertia. Most transformations, and the processes that achieve them, will fail in this era of organisational quakes, as they merely aim to arrive at a new status quo. The following approaches to change or organisational transformation are often tried, and their limitations render them either inaccessible or useless to the people within organisations:

- the prescriptive approach
- the critical mass approach
- the transformational leader.

The prescriptive approach

The prescriptive approach is favoured by some consulting groups. Their approach is to tell the organisation 'this is what everyone must do'. At best, consulting groups may have experiences elsewhere that enable them to make recommendations for action but the prescriptive approach is invariably one of treating the organisation as a machine, one with a design that can be improved. It fails to recognise the Vital Connections that already exist within every organisation.

Typically, the approach is a top-down, roll-out approach to change. The energy dedicated to convincing the executives, who sign the cheques, is rarely matched by a commitment to the people who are vital to make the changes work. In any case, changes made to re-engineer the organisation will not work.

One major organisation re-engineering project, based upon a prescriptive approach and observed by one of the authors for five years, revealed a number of important lessons about problems inherent in re-engineering from this endeavour.

Lack of staff ownership of the change program

To ensure some participation of the organisation's people, project teams were established to develop implementation strategies. The teams selected from the service providers were regarded as a special clique within the organisation. This is also how they came to regard themselves. All attention was focused on their involvement. Line staff were not involved—they were only participants in implementing the project team's work. Distrust and suspicion grew.

Failure to communicate the restructure in meaningful terms

Eighteen months after the restructure started in two pilot units (out of 13), staff were asking what it was all about. At this time, a series of short video messages from the CEO were developed. The CEO restated all the early messages in terms of the benefits to the organisation, without being concrete—for example, 'We're aiming to be Number One in Australia.' The benefits to the staff were not clear, and customer benefits were only vaguely expressed. There was no effort to win the hearts and minds of the employees.

Suspicion about the real agenda

The restructure was initially heralded as a customer service initiative. It was soon regarded by most as a cost-cutting exercise. The retrenchments that occurred within the first 12 months of the pilot just confirmed their suspicions.

Duplication of effort

The project established a couple of pilots, in different states in Australia. In these pilots, there was a massive duplication of effort, due to the absence of a clear communication channel (a Vital Connection), and a lack of broad commitment to a shared goal or preferred future. Accordingly, there was no alignment of the energies of the people involved.

Massive increase in stress and anxiety

Staff involved in the project had an enormous increase in workload and responsibility—with no corresponding pay-off. Staff who were not involved became very worried about their future. The executive and consulting group's focus was on the pilot; the rest of their employees were forgotten. The substantial retrenchments—the who and why—were not explained. Everyone developed their own reasons for why they might be next.

Inappropriate learning programs and support

The restructuring meant a fundamental change in job design. New competencies were identified but these were not developed into learning programs; consequently staff development that directly addressed these new competencies or the restructured jobs was not available when it was needed most.

Promised reward systems didn't appear

New systems of reward/appreciation and recognition were promised as a part of the 'deal'. These were not designed or available until years after the roll-out. The systems, if and when they did arrive, were based upon generating activity around a few goals by using traditional 'carrots and sticks'.

Inappropriate team-building exercises

It was recognised early that team-building was required by the restructuring project teams, and within the new work units. The team-building that occurred relied almost exclusively on experiential activities—simulations and outdoor activities. Links were not established to the goals of the restructure or to the organisation's vision.

Teams did not set work-relevant goals or strategies as a part of the team-building activity. When they returned to work, nothing changed.

Staff resistance

The new job competencies were practised for a month or two but staff did not accept the new status quo. The pilot had to roll-out twice as staff reverted to old and familiar practices.

No one was prepared for failure

The initial areas involved in the restructure became among the lowest performing units in the organisation. (The best performing work units were those that were not involved.) The morale and motivation of people dropped dramatically. The culture went from people working until the job was done, to a 'nine to five' culture almost overnight. The senior managers in the initial pilot were retrenched. No one had planned on failure, or even for a lack of short-term success.

A lack of shared values and vision

In the endeavour to become something known as the Number One in Australia, work units within the organisation competed against each other and failed to share their ideas and best practices. One unit developed a vision statement—to be the 'best in the organisation'. It was finally suggested that they should focus their energies to take aim at the competitors rather than their own company. The vision should be the 'best in their marketplace'.

Transformation

At no stage were the *values* of the restructure expressed, let alone agreed to and broadcast. Each person's role in achieving the goals was not explored or agreed upon.

Blame in the organisation grew
After the initial waves of shock and sympathy wore off, the perception grew that the retrenched deserved their fate. Management did nothing to dispel this. Why should they? It let them off the hook.

People started to make themselves look good by making everyone else look bad. It was rare to hear praise within the organisation.

In the above case, the organisation was treated as a machine. The re-engineering process was accompanied by retrenchments and restructuring of the jobs of the survivors. The process was in the control of managers—the role of Vital Connections was never recognised, apart from some lip service to the 'people being assets'.

No one ever said what the re-engineering was supposed to achieve, so it comes as little surprise that three years after the conclusion of the first roll-out, a report concluded:

'. . . *no material impact on cost ratio* . . .'
'. . . *expense ratio down slightly* . . .'
'. . . *income down* . . .'
'. . . *little improvement anywhere apart from bad debts* . . .'

The organisation's response to the situation was to consider more staff cuts and a greater control of expenses. This organisation is not alone in its experience of re-engineering. The failure of re-engineering and restructuring processes is now epidemic, as noted in many studies.[11]

The prescriptive approach has damaged many of this company's Vital Connections, as it does wherever it is practised. As the approach specifies the 'right' way to go, people are often put down if they are less than full supporters of the change. Trust and respect, energy flows that support the interdependence of everyone, are often irreparably damaged.

Peck's 'real communities', or the organisations that have achieved the extraordinary results reported by Kotter and Heskett, identify an alternative that has not been considered by the architects of organisational restructures and re-engineering.

The great pity is that if the people in charge of the transformation process had seen the organisation as a garden or living organism, the results could have been very different. This is not just the lesson of hindsight. The architects of prescriptive approaches—managers and external consultants—could have heeded the work done by Kurt Lewin in the 1940s. Marvin Weisbord wrote of Lewin's 'priceless insight':

Lewin showed that all problems, even technical and economic, have social consequences that include people's feelings, perceptions of reality, sense of self-worth, motivation, and commitment. It is not given to consultants, for example, to sow the seeds of change (a screwy notion that gets us into trouble), but to discover what seeds are already present and whether they can be grown.[12]

Architects and managers of prescriptive approaches have done their work regardless of the impact they have on the Vital Connection they have with their people. (Discussions at management level about consequences to people in times of turbulence are often restricted to the most humane way to retrench them.) This has fundamental consequences for the future of the organisation.

When they ignore the need to work with Vital Connections, including developing the forces that will pull the organisation towards a preferred future, they change people's perceptions of what is real and alter their commitment and their role within the organisation. They alter what it means to work.

Prescriptive approaches do not work, but even if they did, they would have to be challenged as cynical exercises in power and failures at capturing the energy of people.

The critical mass approach

The critical mass approach suggests that if 'we do this to enough people the organisation will change'. This approach shares many of the characteristics of the prescriptive approach, especially if it is driven by external 'experts'. It may have been an appropriate change model for those organisations in earlier times striving to establish a new status quo. By its nature, the status quo is 'fixed' and the concept of 'unfreezing' one status quo, changing to a new state, and then 'refreezing' to a new status quo was appropriate when a new fixed state was desirable and achievable.[*]

Establishing a new status quo is neither desirable nor achievable today. Organisations have to continually adapt and grow.

The focus on critical mass may be appropriate today only in circumstances as limited as, for example, a product launch. There is little point advertising a new product to the public if the key messages and an operational knowledge about that product have not been received by the majority of service providers within an organisation. But a focus on developing a critical mass rather than developing Vital Connections can be counterproductive to the organisational transformation process.

The basic assumptions behind the focus of developing a critical mass need to be challenged. The approach has been described by trainers:

There is an enormous difference between having 500 different courses with an average of ten people attending each one, and having ten courses with a cumulative average of 500 people attending each one. While the total number of training days is the same, the impact on the organisation could not be more different. If those highly-attended courses are fundamental, building block courses, which develop job skills and inculcate core strategic values, the impact on the whole system can be profound. But without such 'critical mass' generated by wide attendance, the organisational impact of even the finest training program is soon dissipated.

---

[*] Kurt Lewin developed an influential model of change in the early 1950s. His three-step sequential change model involves 'unfreezing' the present behaviour pattern, 'changing' to new behaviour patterns, and then 'refreezing' the new behaviours.

Peter Drucker said that he thinks an organisation must train at least 30 per cent of any group in order to impact the entire group in a meaningful way. We concur with that observation. If a company wishes to develop its sales force, it cannot train only two per cent of them and expect them to go back and transform all the rest.[13]

The assumptions underlying this passage spring from a view of the company as a machine. We would argue—because we have achieved just this—if you want to develop the sales force of a company you *can* start with just 2 per cent of them and expect them to go back and change the rest.

In 1991, a major Australian corporation sent 500 managers through sales training for the right reason—the company needed to grow. As a result a critical mass was achieved (90 per cent of managers completed training), but there was *no increase in sales.* There may be many reasons why it didn't work. Was it the right training? Were they the right people for the program? Was training the solution? Perhaps there were other reasons for the lack of growth that required a different response—an increase in competitor activity, a poor relationship with customers? Did participants understand their sales role? Did participants understand what the management was trying to achieve? Did they agree with the organisation's direction?

Working with Vital Connections is a different matter altogether. By the time the above questions have been answered, the humble 2 per cent may be making more of a difference than the 30 or 90 per cent who attended the training. A Vital Connection is not only *those people who can and want to act directly to speed the transformation,* but also ideas, processes and approaches which on the surface have no immediately apparent, recognisable connection. We have achieved greater results with the 2 per cent who are willing and able to act directly to speed a transformation than we have in the past focusing on building a critical mass.

The starting point
The process or product called 'training' should be recalled—like many others associated with a machine. It gives an organisation a false sense of

security because it knows that it has done 'something'. It has identified some important things to be addressed and it has told the employee that this will be good for them and the organisation.

There is still a role for learning programs within an organisation but the focus must shift from critical mass and 'training' to Vital Connections and learning. It is this shift that allows true transformation to happen. Learning starts with the people who seek out what they need to know, and are given the opportunity, the resources and the support necessary.

The starting point is the people who *can and want to act directly to speed transformation*. If people learn what they decide they need to know, they are more likely to use that learning. Training can be too closely associated with extrinsic rather than intrinsic motivation. Trying to motivate people to learn by attending training because someone else decides that it is important to them will screw up their intrinsic motivation, particularly if they return to work and find no opportunity to implement their new knowledge.

For most of us, learning comes from what we do. It is linked to the Vital Connection people have with their work. Learning involves both action and reflection and an off-the-job program may play a part in this. The quantum leaps in knowledge and performance that are required by organisations today must and will only happen in work groups with a propensity for action and learning together.

While some may still cling to training as a vehicle for improving the job process skills of a mass of people, the changing of behaviours within a culture will never be the result of training. When writing about changing behaviour in corporate cultures, Drucker is not a supporter of the critical mass approach to training.

After defining the results that were needed, he indicated the need for a different perspective when he wrote in 1989:

The next—and most important—step is not *a 'training session' or a management conference, let alone a lecture by the big boss. It is to ask: 'Where within our system are we doing this already?'*[14]

This is looking for, and using, Vital Connections. A Critical Leader finds the energy flowing within the organisation, the seeds for adaptation and growth, and builds on this pre-existing, unchannelled energy.

The transformational leader

If they have a picture of a preferred future, and *if* they do all the right things for their people, working for a transformational leader must be an exhilarating experience.

These are bold 'ifs'. There is no doubting that the person at the top has the greatest ability to influence and direct a transformation. We have only to think of Anita Roddick and The Body Shop or Jack Welch at GE for inspiration, wherever we work. These leaders have the greatest ability to influence the political climate for change. And the person at the top also has the greatest potential to take the organisation down the tube or his or her team to jail.

The 'ifs' have to stand, even though the transformational leader may have both the picture of the preferred future and the commitment to get there. No one at the top was ready for the organisational quakes that hit them in the 1980s and 1990s. And no one person has either the knowledge or the experience to determine the actions necessary for the future.

There is no right answer to organisational transformation and renewal—there never was, there never will be. The only answer is to tap into the energy of other people. Transformational leaders demonstrate that they recognise this.

In 1982, John Kotter found that effective general managers:

- spent 70–90 per cent of their time with other people
- often by-passed the normal chains of command and spent their time with many different people
- asked many questions
- often didn't plan their actions—they reacted to other's initiatives
- were rarely seen to make 'big' decisions.[15]

This is working with Vital Connections.

| Transformation |

In the same year that Kotter published these findings, Jan Carlzon wrote that he spent 'exactly half of [his] working hours "out in the field" talking to SAS employees' and he claimed that 'the great triumph at SAS is that we have unleashed our employees' creativity'.[16]

David Glass, CEO of Walmart, spends two or three days each week in stores talking to some of his almost half a million 'associates'. Almost a decade after Kotter's paper, Jack Welch was to speak of owing every good thing in General Electric to the 'liberation of some individual, some team, or some business'.[17] It is clear that where there is a successful transformational leader, there is a focus on the elements of both Critical Leadership and Vital Connections.

Of the three methods of achieving organisational transformation, working with a transformational leader is the method with some appeal. The truth of the matter is that these people are few and far between. The strength of Critical Leadership and Vital Connections is that the transformational leader is not a prerequisite for success. For most of us, we have to work with the leaders we have, and, if we are committed to building a preferred future with our people, we cannot afford to give up if the political climate or the leader at the top is not 'right'.

What does it take to succeed?

The beginning is to know your organisation as a living organism with a 'shifting harmony of patterns'. From this 'knowing', you are able to develop your preferred picture for the future. This will change the meaning of your working life. You must *find* the people who are willing and able to change their picture of the organisation and its future. They are there in great numbers, because it is in our nature to be of service in our work.

It is here that your work as a Critical Leader begins.

4.
Meaning

*People who find their lives meaningful usually have a goal that is challenging enough to take up all their energies, a goal that can give significance to their lives. We may refer to this process as achieving **purpose** . . . a unified purpose is what gives meaning to life.*

Mihaly Csikszentmihalyi[1]

The most important issue facing organisations today is redefining the meaning of work in an era of turbulence and organisational quakes. 'What does it mean to work here?', and 'What is the reason for our existence?' are fundamental questions for people and their organisations. The perspective from which an organisation is viewed by employees will ultimately determine their answers.

In the machine organisation, people are a resource and have an established role in one or a number of processes. They are defined by their jobs: 'I am a . . .', and their contentment comes from a fixed status quo. In the garden organisation, alive to its societal, technological and economic environment, people are the driving force of the organisation. They determine the preferred future of the organisation and they are involved in Vital Connections rather than processes. The nature of their work will continually change as the organisation transforms itself. People will define themselves through their sense of self and the purpose of their work: 'I am (name) and I help . . .' Their happiness will stem from the harmony that is possible when work has a purpose and that purpose is attainable through their commitment and endeavours.

Defining purpose

If we focus on doing things and checking them, we have missed the opportunity to maximise the incredible value that organisations are capable of producing. Is performance defined by activity—or actually moving forward? Is the purpose simply to do something—or to get somewhere? Is it to screw pieces together—or to make things grow?

Managers have defined performance in terms of goals or targets in the belief that what gets measured gets done. What gets measured may indeed get done, as many companies that use sales targets to measure performance have found. But we worked with one company whose total sales were matched by the number of customer defections. It was a zero sum game.

Contrast this with the courier company that decided everyone's role was to do whatever it took to prevent customer defections. This meant that drivers, sales representatives and dispatchers received the authority to look after customers, even if it meant authorising credits or refunds. All the manager asked was that a reason be given for the corrective action, so that the root causes of problems could be identified.

The manager and the Critical Leader are both concerned with improving performance. Managers have traditionally defined performance as a function of two variables—ability and motivation. This has not proved to be adequate for times of transformation. Critical Leaders respond to a new model of performance, which incorporates a new variable—Accuracy of Role Perception. Performance is examined in greater detail in Chapter 9.

Assisting people with their role perceptions does not mean defining their jobs into task statements. Rather, it is clarifying the minimum critical specifications. It also incorporates their role as a member of a team, as a learner and contributor to the learning of the others, and as a champion of continuous adaptation that improves the way the organisation does business.

Clarifying the role of people at all levels through the model of Critical Leadership is an essential step towards providing a meaningful purpose to their work. Another crucial step is to help them to focus on five aspects of leadership, implicitly incorporating many of the concepts of Critical Leadership with their Vital Connections. James Kouzes and Barry Posner's landmark book, *The Leadership Challenge*, outlines the behaviours and practices of leaders. The great value of Kouzes and Posner's research and application is that it lays to rest the views that there are 'born leaders' or that leadership is contingent upon charisma. Kouzes and Posner surveyed over 5000 managers who achieved 'extraordinary' results, along with their people, to identify the common practices which contributed to their success. They conclude that leadership:

. . . is not the private reserve of a few charismatic men and women. It is a process ordinary managers use when they are bringing forth the best from themselves and others.[2]

The five practices of the exemplary leader encompassed activities that were engaged in for 80 per cent of their time. These practices reveal a pattern for leaders to apply to their own organisation. Each practice has two basic strategies. They are enumerated in Table 4.1.

Table 4.1 The five practices and ten commitments of leaders

Challenging the process

People do their best when there is a chance to improve the way things are

- Search for opportunities to change, grow, innovate and improve
- Experiment, take risks, learn from accompanying mistakes

Meaning

Inspiring a shared vision

There is no sure pathway to the future but leaders motivate their people with a sense of purpose

- Envision an uplifting and ennobling future
- Enlist others in a common vision by appealing to their values, interests, hopes and dreams

Enabling others to act

Leaders know that they need a team to get extraordinary things done in an organisation

- Foster collaboration by promoting co-operative goals and building trust
- Strengthen others—share information and power, increase their discretion and visibility

Modelling the way

Leaders have a high set of values about how employees and customers should be treated. They have principles that make their organisation unique and exceptional

- Set an example for others by behaving in ways consistent with your stated values
- Plan small wins that promote consistent progress and build commitment

Encouraging the heart

Working in a time of change is hard work and success can be a long way ahead. Leaders encourage others and take real pride in the success of their teams

- Recognise individual contributions to the success of every project
- Celebrate team accomplishments regularly

Source: © 1995 James M. Kouzes and Barry Z. Posner. From *The Leadership Challenge: How To Keep Getting Extraordinary Things Done in Organizations*, San Francisco: Jossey-Bass, p. 14. All rights reserved. Reprinted with permission.

(People can analyse their own behaviour according to these practices, as well as gaining feedback from their colleagues. Kouzes and Posner have designed the Leadership Practices Inventory for this purpose.)

Strategies for developing meaning

Oh good, nobody here but people.
Mrs Veta Simmons[3]

In major organisational shifts the cultural carpet is ripped out from under the people. They have joined an organisation because of a perceived alignment or congruence of personal values and organisational culture. When the leaders of an organisation transform the processes or the focus, they create a new blueprint. However this is often not enough as success is most likely to come through developing an adaptive culture.

People now know, after their experience of the last five or six years, that restructure follows restructure, redesign follows redesign. While the human side of change has never been handled well, it is in danger of being neglected altogether as the leaders of organisations focus on the perceived 'easy bits'—the processes, strategies and structures.

It is essential to prepare people for a life within an ever-changing organisation. A continuously adaptive organisation will never be effective without the agreement of the people. The greater the awareness and participation, the more the acceptance and support of the change. Most organisations fail in achieving effective restructures. Why? Typically, because more time is spent on the management of *things* than on the impact of change upon *people*. Establishing the purpose and values behind the change, and changing the behaviours at the uppermost levels of management, is critical for effective transformation.

It is easy to spend time on re-engineering processes, and redesigning structures. These are tangible things with which we can grapple. It is difficult to tackle issues around oneself and the people within the organisation. It is hard to focus on the shifting cultural fabric of the organisation. Yet neglecting this blocks transformation.

A strategy that looks after the needs of the people needs to be followed during the continual organisational shifts. This strategy takes several critical areas into account. The organisation's Critical Leaders:

- recognise and plan for the needs of the people
- communicate a clear picture of a 'preferred' future for the organisation and its people
- focus on self-adaptation
- create and facilitate the flow of information and feelings
- build time into the plan, allowing for help for the people.

Planning for the needs of the people

There are many signs to watch for when helping people cope with transformation. A common error is that of pulling people into the process before recognising and appreciating the stages through which they will go. Change models suggest that particular attention be paid to the steps of ending, transition and beginning. Organisations start with the new beginning, thereby failing to provide the people with time to deal with the loss of the context, the end of the affinity between themselves and the organisation they know, and which is a fundamental and important part of their lives. William Bridges wrote:

Endings are, let's remember, experiences of dying. They are ordeals, and sometimes they challenge so basically our sense of who we are that we all believe they will be the end of us.[4]

Organisations tend not to appreciate that change is primarily about people's emotions, and not processes. Failure to identify and manage the emotions leads to a dysfunctional workforce. This results in either a failed or ineffective transformation program.

Failing to deal with emotional responses to change increases the ambiguity of direction and meaning. Ambiguity during a reorganisation program destroys confidence and the job concentration of employees. It is critical for leaders to know what the reactions of their people are, not what they say. It is equally critical to allow time and space for people to work through their reactions.

The cardinal rule in dealing with change is that where people come down is where they come down. Their reactions, whatever they are, are normal and natural for them given their experiences and the general circumstances.[5]

People issues involve a clear identification of the state of people's emotions, allowance for a period to work through feelings before starting the next 'new' thing and a plan for caring for the people through this period of genuine emotional trauma.

Those orchestrating the transformation may choose to begin the process by 'borrowing' behavioural actions consistent with the established objectives. The 'borrowing' must be based on a clearly communicated picture of a shared and 'preferred' future and stated desirable values which are consistent with that vision. This behaviour must be modelled by management or the people will know that the change is not serious.

Communicating a picture of a 'preferred' future

Leaders in organisations undergoing major shifts often fail to recognise the extent of personal trauma within the workforce. This failure often results in the people refusing to follow the leaders in the transformation.

In order to minimise this effect there must be clear communication. Limerick and Cunnington suggest in *Managing the New Organisation* that in organisations experiencing deep cultural transformation the management of meaning must take dominance over the management of process, or things. Organisational development practitioners support the critical nature of managing the context of transformation. Without clearly communicating the context or meaning of the reinvention, the most that can be expected is short-term, transitory change.

Context, or meaning of the working environment, affects how we observe work and what we think of the work we do. A shift of as little as 15 per cent of a person's job function fundamentally alters their understanding of the meaning of work. This shift in context creates difficulty in grasping the point of the business.

Context sets the stage; being pertains to whether the actor lives the part or merely goes through the motions. Organisations and the people in them are being something all the time. On occasion, we describe them as 'conservative'... or 'resistant to change'. Trouble is, aside from casual generalisations, we concentrate mostly on what we are doing and let being fend for itself.[6]

Without an easily understandable new context or meaning, blockages inhibit the effectiveness of the transformation. Given a chance, people use any means possible to maintain the 'old' way. Establishing the context for transformation means really understanding what the people do or do not know.

Focusing on self-adaptation

Change programs often fail to be optimally effective because executives do not simultaneously transform the context in which they operate and make decisions. Research indicates that executives tend to reject philosophical thoughts concerning themselves as leaders of change. Leaders are often unable to shift the context of their decision-making to align with the emerging adaptive nature of the 'New Organisation'. It should not be assumed that leaders have an easier time adapting to the change simply because they are the 'leaders'.

Gross, Pascales and Athos in the *Harvard Business Review* state:

. . . we have found, particularly in senior executives, an unwillingness to think rigorously and patiently about themselves or their ideas. We often find senior executives perched like a threatened aristocracy, entitled, aloof, and sensing doom.[7]

Establishing universally meaningful goals speeds organisational transformations because everyone has had a say in what it is they are attempting to accomplish—'we have established our commonality of purpose and have negotiated a mutually accurate perception of roles'. The organisation then has accessed all of the available information in the determination of its goal.

As noted earlier, M. Scott-Peck refers to true communities, where people can 'communicate with one another on an ever more deep and authentic level'.[8] Such a need is also recognised by Kouzes and Posner who use the term 'creating shared values' as the means of finding the common ground within an organisation:

One of the most common mistakes made in attempting to create shared values is announcing which are most important and should guide the department (or company). This approach may have worked in the old command and control hierarchies, in which managers told and sold values. It does not work in today's more diverse work environment. Instead, leaders must cast the net widely to capture the broadest possible understanding of constituents' values. Having listened, leaders and constituents must then learn to speak with one voice.[9]

When driving transformation, Critical Leaders must model the way. Contradictory signals occur all too often and add to an already high degree of ambiguity.

Critical Leaders endeavour to clearly understand the new organisation, and they focus on performing key tasks in order to lead the people successfully in the shift. The five practices that were shared by effective leaders in the US and Australia need to be incorporated into the design of the emerging organisation (Table 4.1, pages 62–3). They are:

- challenge the process
- inspire a shared vision
- enable others to act
- model the way
- encourage the heart.[10]

Facilitating the flow of information

Communication issues are probably at the root of effectiveness. Issues to be tackled include: what to say, when to say it, how to say it, people's perceptions of what was said, what the organisation is saying by not saying anything and what messages the network is really receiving.

The assumption of the task force is, 'We haven't said anything yet, so we're not really communicating. We haven't sent any messages.' But the opposite is true.[11]

Despite a constantly changing environment during periods of discontinuity, the clearer the goals and intentions of the organisation, the less ambiguity people feel about their lives. The less open and honest (as perceived by those who receive it) communication about what is really occurring, the greater the likelihood of damaging underground rumours.

Communication is what ultimately determines whether the organisation gains the hearts and minds of the people, or simply their backs and arms. It is a common experience for people simply not to accept the new designed processes, no matter how good, because they have no sense of ownership of their jobs, of the changes. Leaders must 'be the message', and that message must be carried within a clearly understood context. Failure on this point leads to an ultimate lack of buy-in and effectiveness. It lengthens the time needed to recover the 'health' of the people.

Building time and support into the plan

Time is critical to the entire issue of effectiveness. In the rush to beat the competition, organisations tackle restructuring with detailed implementation plans for processes, organisational structure and work roles. Restructuring plans must also provide clear road maps which place human issues at the pinnacle of the change list. These road maps must address:

- the amount of time it takes for everyone in the organisation to understand why the transformation is required
- people who will be reluctant to embrace the transformation—those who are content with the status quo and those who are clearly unhappy with the organisation, its direction or leadership
- identification of the connections vital for success of transformation—those people at all levels of the organisation who are Vital Connections, people who can make or break the initiatives
- a communication plan that:

    - initially makes everyone aware of the nature and need for transformation
    - informs everyone about the nature and extent of the transformation
    - provides opportunities for everyone to discuss how the transformation will affect them

- the amount of time that can be allotted to the grieving process, and the actions that will be taken to shorten this time
- the amount of time to be devoted to executives learning to transform their context, the meaning of their job, and actually making these changes—staff should be able to see executives adopt new behaviours before they are expected to change themselves.

Table 4.2 identifies some of the prerequisites for engaging and helping the people with transformation—providing the meaning for the transformation.

| Meaning |

Table 4.2 Prerequisites for providing meaning

1. How often do you discuss your organisation's preferred future?
2. Do the executives in your organisation share and discuss with their people a picture of the preferred future?
3. How often do your people discuss the preferred future?
4. Are there regularly scheduled forums and workshops which focus on the continually shifting context of the organisation?
5. How do your people feel about organisational shifts and change? Are they:
    - resistors?
    - victims?
    - thrivers?
    - creators?
6. Is there a shared philosophy of leadership in your organisation?
7. Does *everyone* in your organisation have free access to all the information they wish to have?
8. Can everyone in your organisation explain how the transformation will affect them and what their 'new' work will look like?

The transformation of organisations has only just begun. The future is unimaginable in the present. In order to deal with this moving future it is critical to establish the context for continuous transformation.

Discovery

Meaning

The machine	*The garden*
Define activity	Define purpose
Assume the co-operation of the people	Recognise and plan for the needs of people
Communicate changes in processes	Communicate a 'preferred future'
Focus on command and control	Focus on self-adaptation
Control the flow of information	Facilitate the flow of information
Meet unrealistic process deadlines	Build time into the plan

5.
Directions

As discontinuities hit organisations and create crisis, they either reignite the old vision, or ignite a new one.

Limerick and Cunnington[1]

What should you be spending your time on each and every day? What are the things that you indicate to your employees, directly or indirectly, that they should be spending their time on? This chapter begins by asking you to first establish how you spend your time. The purpose of this simple exercise is to determine the nature of your daily focus at work. For this exercise, picture yourself with the person at work with whom you come into the most contact each day. List the five most frequently discussed topics.

Think now of people in your workplace with whom you come in contact only infrequently. List the five questions you are most likely to ask them.

Now categorise your list. How many topics or questions focus on the goals of the organisation, or the broad context of what people are trying to do? How many may be thought of as detail-focused questions—those that get down to the nitty-gritty of what must happen in order to keep work moving?

Is your focus on the big picture—the goals of the organisation, communicating the message, seeing how you can be of assistance in keeping interpretations of the organisational map in focus? Or is your focus on the minute details of the what and how, the checking up, the gears of the organisational drivers?

Do you believe your focus is centred on the truly important aspects of the organisation, or only on those easy-to-see-and-correct concerns?

Mountains and maps

It is important to have a clear understanding of the different effects of focusing on the overall picture or the daily detail. It is important to make a conscious choice about what to focus on, and when.

This is an area of confusion in many organisations. What often masquerades as a 'time management' problem is really a more basic problem with distinguishing between fundamental goals and organisational detail. You will always be busy—the question is whether it is on the big or the little things, on the mountains and maps, or on the footpaths.

The importance of 'big' things became apparent on reading *First Things First* by Covey, Merrill and Merrill.[2] They relate a wonderful story that reinforces the idea of focusing on the important aspects. A training instructor places some fist-sized rocks in a wide-mouthed jar, and his audience assumes that it is full. Then he dumps some gravel into the jar, which filters down between the rocks. But the jar is still not 'full'. He adds a bucket of sand to the jar, filling all the little spaces. Finally, he adds a quart of water to the jar. After some puzzling the moral to the story emerges: Put the big rocks in the jar first. Why? If you don't put the big rocks in first, you'll never fit them in.

All around organisations arguments may be heard: 'If everyone could stop spending so much time on the big picture and just did what they were supposed to do, we could get the job done.' Or, alternatively, 'If everyone would just stop running around doing things for a minute and focus on what we were trying to accomplish . . .'

How much time should people in an organisation spend on contemplating the mountain and studying the map (vision and values), and how much time on watching the steps of the footpath (details) ahead? Many consulting groups preach that if everyone is focused on the tasks that they need to do, including the new ones that have developed as a result of re-engineering or restructuring, then the organisation will tick. (This is a blind, fanatic belief that somehow we will find a means of making Taylorism workable.) The prescriptions organisations then follow focus upon finding methods of motivating people to do those detail-oriented tasks efficiently and effectively. People will be offered carrots or threatened with sticks in order to get them to do their job, however meaningless it may have become (especially after the job they knew has been ripped out from under them). This pursuit of 'Taylorism made workable' is equated with the holy grail of organisational efficiency.

A balance must be achieved. *Not* sticking to the footpaths can trip you up and they must be watched. But without understanding the mountain and following the map you can easily find yourself running in a circle. All the steps may get taken, but they won't take you anywhere.

Senior management of organisations may be constantly preoccupied with minute details. Is this because they do not trust the people in their employ to be competent? Is it because they haven't a clue how to focus beyond the daily detail? Is it because they are convinced that if their focus is on the detail of things, the big picture will take care of itself? Who is plotting the course, and who is fixing the engines? If one person can do both jobs, why have employees and managers?

Alternatively, what is the value of the people within an organisation who spend their time dreaming of the future? How does it possibly help to bring cash in the door today if management is always speaking of the organisation in five or ten years time? Are they making any relevant contribution? Do they spend their time dreaming because they do not know how to get things done?

Critical Leaders have familiarised themselves with the mountain and the map and communicate this information to everyone in the organisation continuously. The map (our purpose) shows us the picture of the mountain (our goal) that we are attempting to climb. Critical Leaders also know when to deal with the steps on the footpath, and when to let others deal with them. They focus their capabilities on getting the entire puzzle together.

During organisational quakes, Critical Leadership is about finding ways to get the entire organisation focused on what is important. Given the opportunity to observe the terrain ahead of time, how many explorers would not jump at the chance? If you were the leader of the expedition, would you not share this information with all members of your party, asking them to study it fully? Would you not hold a briefing session to discuss the various alternative plans for the expedition's success? In fact, how many people who were not fully aware of the difficulties of the journey would be welcome to join you on a perilous quest?

On such an expedition, there may be a call for people with special knowledge or abilities. Do you believe that the leader of the expedition should become an expert in all of these, or will they simply have to develop trust in other expedition members in order to move ahead?

Organisational transformation is a journey that may be plotted ahead of time. Obstacles both anticipated and unanticipated are sure to spring up, attempting to block passage. The more radical the transformation, the greater the probability of unanticipated obstacles. People along for the journey begin to suggest turning back—perhaps the quest is not worth achieving? Perhaps the status quo is the place to strive for, no higher than ground zero? But aiming for balance—ground zero—has taken us nowhere.

It is not good enough to have a few people within the organisation who understand the expedition plans, the unquestioning majority relegated to fulfilling intricately designed tasks. Organisations are moving rapidly over uncharted territory. Confining the organisation's people to the footpaths without the maps dooms the organisation to be unresponsive to obstacles. And in a world of high-speed change, this is a recipe for disaster. If each member of the organisation does not clearly understand the map, they cannot contribute the energy required to travel towards the organisation's goal. They may be spending precious energy dealing with things that are fundamentally unimportant. While we clearly need efficient attention to detail, it must be the detail that supports the preferred future of the organisation.

Alignment and the road to zero

Most organisations appear to find it extremely difficult to think of the alignment of strategy, structure and processes in any fashion other than static. Margaret Wheatley tells us how as children we relish the continuous motion of '. . . energies in search of adventure'.[3] As we grow up, we lose our sense of discovery, and sadly, when we come to work within organisations we are implicitly told to check that spirit at the door each day. Wheatley describes this loss:

It seems that the very experiences these children seek out are ones we avoid: disequilibrium, novelty, loss of control, surprise. These make for a good playground, but for a dangerous life. We avoid these things so much that if an organisation were to take the form of a teeter-totter, we'd brace it up at both ends, turning it into a straight plank.[4]

She points out that definitions of equilibrium appear to be quite negative: 'A condition in which the result of all activity is zero.' Zero activity in an organisation can produce an extremely undesirable state.

I've observed the search for organisational equilibrium as a sure path to institutional death, a road to zero trafficked by fearful people.[5]

The alignment of purposes, goals and processes within an organisation should be regarded as continuous and dynamically adaptive, with ebbs and flows. Perhaps a more apt word for the shifting alignments of context and details in organisations is syzygy.

When there is a syzygetic approach within the organisation, there should be the greatest possible opportunity to make real progress towards a flexible preferred future. Aside from providing a great new Scrabble word, syzygy may help provide alignment of a dynamic nature. The planets are not always aligned. They travel at different rates, on different paths. But periodically they pull together. And all the time there is a flow of energy, even when the system is not in equilibrium.

To stay viable, open systems maintain a state of non-equilibrium, keeping the system off balance so that it can change and grow. They participate in an active exchange with their environment, using what is there for their own renewal. Every organism in nature, including us, behaves that way.[6]

A state of static alignment in an organisation is neither desirable nor ultimately achievable. Endeavours to create this kind of state within an organisation are the product of the machine mentality.

The moment when all the planetary forces pull together is a predictable event. Organisational alignment is not something that can exist on a daily basis. It is something that may be planned for, and taken advantage of, in order to get the most out of transformational quakes.

Initiatives designed to assist organisations adapt and grow must be crafted so that while they may be of differing scales, implemented at differing rates, periodically goals and processes create a syzygetic pull which catapults the organisation to a new phase in its journey.

It is also important for the organisation to take information from its environment in the times when it is not in equilibrium, and use that knowledge to plan for the time when all the energies are in alignment.

Vision and values

. . . a vision articulates a view of a realistic, credible, attractive future for the organisation, a condition that is better in some important ways than what now exists.[7]

Directions

Those involved with organisational change and improvement have tried to provide focus in organisations by establishing the organisation's vision and values. This is simply an attempt to show where the organisation is going, and what important things need to be remembered on the path to getting there. In some form, vision and values are crucial to the effective transformation of any organisation. The people of the organisation are the only conduit along which to move through the present towards the future. They must have a picture of where they are going.

In *The Leadership Challenge*, Kouzes and Posner write:

Until recently, vision was not part of the management lexicon . . . Currently scholarly work on leadership has made us aware of the importance of leadership vision.[8]

Again, in Limerick and Cunnington:

More controlled studies, such as those of Niehof et al., support the conclusion that 'inspiring a shared vision' is related to job satisfaction and organisational commitment among employees.[9]

And one of the key leadership practices determined by the extensive research of Kouzes and Posner is 'inspiring a shared vision'. All available information suggests that we work better, are happier in our work and are more committed to organisational well-being when we have a clear understanding of the mountain and the map. However, organisational managers and change agents have failed in the task of 'inspiring a shared vision'.

Anecdotal evidence suggests that many people within organisations do not know what to do with corporate visions or values. While the use of vision and values as drivers for change may have had a positive effect on a few organisations, most organisations have blown the credibility factor of their 'vision'. People typically accept the stated values of the executive level as just that: the stated values. They provide no imperative for action.

Impaired vision and the preferred future

There are several reasons that transformation driven by vision and values has not appeared to speed the transformation process, or increased the success rate of corporate reinventions. Instead of 'visions' we have found that it is much more successful to develop with people at all levels of the organisation the picture of the future that they would 'prefer' for the organisation.

Vision statements rarely motivate and the ideal they present is too distant for people to relate to. Everyone, however, knows what the organisation *is*, and what it *should be*. We ask them to identify what *is* and what *should be*, and to work towards their preferred future. Each person's picture of a 'preferred future' will contain individual elements; they will all share a desire for a more fulfilling workplace.

In *Roses and Rust* we talk about 'visions' as they currently are understood and used—we refer to 'preferred futures' as it is used when we work with people to create the organisation as a garden.

Communicating the preferred future

Communicating the preferred future means pointing out where the organisation is going, and what is important in getting there. Communicating the preferred future should give everyone within the organisation a glimpse of the mountain.

Within an organisation experiencing only incremental shifts, this may be enough to keep everyone in the organisation moving along the same path.

However, in times of organisational quakes, considerable problems arise in the traditional communication of vision and values.

People don't routinely buy into a new set of values handed down to them by memo or meeting notes, and few organisations spend time in communicating their new vision and values to each person individually.

There are some notable exceptions, such as the major Australian retailer which has taken each and every member of the organisation through a workshop on the meaning of their new mission statement before it was released to the public. The Ritz-Carlton is another organisation where the actions of each member speak of a common cause.

Avoiding conflict with 'ancient truths'

Whether or not these are articulated anywhere, all organisations have an implied vision and values. They are what the people of the organisation understand working there to be all about.

If an organisation attempts to transform itself with new statements of values and visions which are incongruent with employees' existing knowledge of 'the truth of the matter', without addressing these ancient truths, then conflict and scepticism can result. Members of the organisation may not believe in the possibility of new values and vision working effectively within the organisation.

Who owns the preferred future?

The stated vision and values may be regarded, perhaps correctly, as those of the executive group within the organisation, rather than those of the people. If people are expected to agree and act upon this new map of the organisational journey, without active input and debate, then it will not be surprising if they ignore it, reject it or refuse to consider it their own preferred future.

Avoiding hypocrisy and double standards

The preferred future and the practices to achieve it must be continually and consistently modelled and reinforced by the executive group. It has been suggested in some organisations that the vision and values are for the executive group to determine—and for everyone else to apply. If people feel that they are expected to demonstrate values that managers do not exhibit, then resistance will inevitably emerge.

Techniques for practical application

Potential leaders and employees may not know how to meaningfully apply the vision and values. This may stem partially from the failure to clearly communicate on an individual level, and partly, as Limerick and Cunnington suggest, because:

We are only just beginning to understand the management of meaning. But we have taken a major step in that direction. That step has been to understand that the techniques used for managing meaning during conditions of discontinuous change are different from those required during periods of consolidation.[10]

We need to commit ourselves to learning the new techniques for communicating and manifesting purpose in the workplace.

These are some of our impressions of the difficulties and issues of using vision and values to drive organisational shift. How well do you believe your organisation handles the inculcation of its vision and values?

What kinds of questions do you ask as you wander around within the organisation? Do you ask people how they have helped to deliver the vision of the organisation today, how what they do on a daily basis will enable the organisation to realise its vision? How have the organisational values been upheld today? What were the problems in upholding the organisational values? Do the values seem consistent with the vision? With process and procedure?

Understanding the mountains and maps means consistently asking questions which draw the theory and practice of vision and values closer together. However, as stated above, there are many difficult issues and bad experiences already surrounding the use of vision and values to drive organisational transformations. Developing a shared picture of the preferred future is a way in which perceptions of what *is* and what *should be* are expressed and then brought together. As many people as possible within the organisation should be involved in determining and validating the organisation's preferred future and the means of accomplishing its related goals. The goals must be those of the whole organisation, and not of the executive group. We must move towards collectively negotiated goals. The map in the leaders' hands must become the common map. It is imperative that all members of the organisation continually challenge each other to ensure that everything they are doing is consistent with the eventual attainment of the goal.

The benefits of involvement

There are several important benefits resulting from the entire organisation determining the mountain and the map.

Independent and committed employees

Limerick and Cunnington point to the new type of worker coming into organisations today. They speak of the collaborative individuals who are '... emancipated by discontinuity, empowered by knowledge and driven by values'.[11] These are not people who believe in 'my organisation right or wrong'. These are the people who have a growing sense of their worth and the self-confidence to support that sense.

This new person in the workforce is challenging the way organisations move towards the future. Because of their willingness to change from job to job in pursuit of interesting work, they create pressure on the organisation to share information. These people are beginning to consider work as what they do, and employment as a negotiated contract of where they do it.

This creates a threat to existing methods of goal setting, as well as to other aspects of employment in organisational shifts. At the same time, there is also a new type of casual worker, one who will hold several casual jobs at the same time. This has come about because of the need to create our own security. Many people, having gone through a period where organisational re-engineering translates directly into more job losses, do not care to be solely reliant on the perceived whims of the organisation for the continuation of their employment.

By necessity, these people will create an attitude shift towards the leaders of organisations. It will no longer be enough to set the direction and the jobs of the organisation and tell the people what they must do. As Limerick and Cunnington point out, we are beginning to experience a generation of employees who feel free to say 'no'.

This can help the organisation to grow and adapt in meaningful ways. The simple fact that more and more of the people within an organisation are 'willing to walk' if the organisation does not come up to their standards mandates the inclusion of those very people in setting the organisation's direction. It is the only way that people will feel committed to seeing the shift through.

Commonality of purpose

People must be allowed the freedom to express what it does mean to work for the organisation, and what they believe it should mean to work for the organisation. It is critical for the leaders in the organisation to allow the airing of the people's definitions of what it means to work there. This becomes the method of creating an environment where people begin to feel motivated and feel as if they can contribute to the cause. It also begins the airing of many organisational truths. The process involves everyone contributing to the drawing of the map and the making of the paths—focusing organisational energy in order to transform.

Footpaths and steps . . .

Footpaths are the tasks we perform as individuals—both separately and collaboratively. While the mountain and map focus organisational energy, the footpaths and steps focus and energise the individual. The syzygy of transformation exists when organisational and individual energy are maximised. The inappropriate focus by leaders on how steps are taken on the footpaths stops effective transformations cold.

We need to also realise that we are being forced into allowing individuals the freedom to do the work we have asked them to do. If we indeed want the best people to be members of our organisation we must not interfere with their performance of the tasks we have asked of them. They will walk if they are not happy.

Are you managing the checklists and making sure not only that all the tasks are performed, but they are performed in a prescribed fashion? Is this how your organisation approaches the details? Or are you focusing on the development of the people, so that they are comfortable determining how the tasks are accomplished and feel free to let everyone know if the task is not focused on maximising the individual and organisational energy?

Someone else, like my manager, focusing too minutely on how my energy is expended in accomplishing my job begins to feel like they want to control me. When I am being controlled I begin to feel that I as an individual am irrelevant to the task, and I lose interest in the task. You, as my manager, are no longer provided with maximum use of my energy. I will simply supply you with the minimum required so that you leave me alone.

So the mountain and map lets the individual understand the importance, relevance and fit of the work they and the organisation mutually agree to undertake; the footpaths and steps are the individual's way of making a contribution. The steps and choice of footpath must be left to the individual!

In order to successfully manage the mountains and maps and the footpaths and steps we must learn, as Margaret Wheatley says, to 'trust in the unfolding dance of order'. The approach to managing the details of an organisation must radically change from the command and control approach so many of us have as our management paradigm.

We are no longer being permitted by individuals to treat them as simple parts of the organisational machinery. The competitive nature of the business world will no longer allow us the luxury of treating individuals as parts of the corporate machine. Competitive advantage is gained from the freeing of the individual's capacity to contribute value to the organisation, rather than managing the individual by monitoring the steps on the footpaths.

To be competitive we must let the jobs out of the boxes we have spent years stuffing them into. Margaret Wheatley comments:

It is both sad and ironic that we have treated organisations like machines, acting as though they were dead when all this time they've been living open systems capable of self-renewal. We have magnified the tragedy by treating one another as machines, believing the only way we could motivate others was by pushing and prodding them into action, overcoming entropy by the sheer force of our own energy.[12]

In organisational transformations it is imperative to acknowledge that it is the individual, the person, who will or will not perform. As individuals we are capable of self-organising, of understanding how to make decisions, of understanding when we need help and where to get it from when progress becomes difficult.

We are rediscovering our ability to help; we are seeking out managers who are mentors and coaches. Critical Leaders help others discover how to be the best they can be; it is about creating an environment which allows the individual to devote maximum energy to the quest, because it is meaningful to them. It is the individuals who best know how to organise their own work efficiently to contribute to the organisation's goals.

Citizens of the organisation

Some organisations are moving away from rigid organisational structures and job descriptions. They have realised that rigid structures and jobs limit everyone's potential. Adaptive organisations have an ability to change their shape willingly and quickly based upon an ever-changing interaction—their Vital Connection—with the environment. Capabilities of an organisation must be organised as required to meet the demands of the environment. Structures must be dissolved as easily and as painlessly as they are built. People should understand that this is the way the organisation will work. Such adaptability of a complex system can only happen when everyone in the organisation agrees to the purposes and goals.

Have you yet recognised the new rules of the working game? Limerick and Cunnington warn us that 'the real battle is the one taking place between the individual and the organisation itself'.[13] In the past decade, organisations appear to have done everything possible to remove people's desire to do the work for an organisation. They have trashed the concept of corporate loyalty. They have rationalised, downsized, restructured, retrenched—even fired!—employees. People believe that restructuring is just one more way for the 'top team' to maintain the power structure the way it is.

The new worker is telling us that they will sign on for only as long as they find worthwhile pursuits. The climb is no longer focused up the corporate ladder. According to Limerick and Cunnington:

The organisation provides a learning place for the development of shared values and beliefs among its participants. These values and assumptions become part of the world views of their participants. A paradigm shift in organisations therefore brings with it a new world view, a new set of expectations about the way people should relate to each other, and a new set of values and aspirations.[14]

Taylorism will not be an effective way to transform your organisation. We are witnessing the progressive demise of the good organisational citizen, or the good soldier.

In this battle for power between the individual and institutions, collaborative individuals are slowly winning.

Citizenship, of organisations or society, must be redefined in terms of belonging to a community that is bonded by a duty of care and a commitment to building a preferred future. The leaders of an organisation, the caretakers of its health, well-being and future prosperity no longer have the luxury of a choice. They *cannot* manage the how of the details—they *must* provide people with the resources for personal and professional improvement as those people perceive the need.

Empowerment

Empowerment falls into a similar category as vision and values. That is, it is 'flavour of the month', something we give every impression of being committed to; but something that in any given conversation is mutually misunderstood.

It is also a term that appears to strike terror in the minds of the left brain managers so prevalent within corporations. Visions of everyone running around doing anything they feel like pop into the minds of many managers when they consider the ramifications of empowerment. Yet it is the only way the 'new worker' will accept the working contract. They are telling organisations, 'Give me room to do the work you asked me to do. If I mess it up get rid of me, but I'll stay within the negotiated borders and surpass all of your expectations if you stay out of the way.'

This is the behaviour that the workers in organisations are demanding, if you want their assistance in ensuring the success of transformations. One of the five leadership practices that people expect of leaders is 'enabling others to act'. It seems so simple, but occurs seldom. (It is also the practice in which Australian managers seem to be weakest.)

Anecdotal evidence suggests that the more desperate the organisation—forced to change or die—the more the organisation disables the actions of others. This is the time that the workers begin to refer to the organisation as belonging to the managers, and not to themselves.

Again, the management of the footpaths and steps deals with trust and faith and admissions of areas where we simply do not know everything. Critical Leadership during transformational quakes tells us to help, but not to interfere.

Discovery

Directions

The machine	The garden
No one asks the question 'What does it mean to work in our organisation?'	Everyone is involved in a dialogue about what it means to work in our organisation
A few are involved in developing the map for the future	Everyone is involved in developing the map for the future
A few experts and managers have the map	Everyone has the map
A few people understand the map	Everyone understands the map

Roses and Rust

The machine	*The garden*
There is a focus on either goals OR the details	There is a focus on goals AND the details
The organisational structure is fixed and restructures occur from time to time	The organisational structure is fluid and adapts to meet needs
People do what they are told to do, even if they don't like it	People do what needs to be done and they do what they think is the right thing to do
People have no authority	People are enabled
People define themselves by the tasks they do	People define themselves by how they participate in Vital Connections and/or help people

6.
Connections

The world of the quark has everything to do with a jaguar circling in the night.

Arthur Sze[1]

Currently, the approach of organisations to control through bureaucracies, chains of command and regulations makes simple things complex, while the things that should be simple, such as the meaning of work, are rarely addressed satisfactorily, if at all.

In *Productive Workplaces*, Weisbord describes the learning curve of organisations over this century. In 1900 experts were called in to solve problems ('scientific management'). The 1950s was the era of 'participative management', which advocated everyone solving the problems. Around 1965 experts discovered 'systems thinking' and started improving systems for other people. Now organisations need experts *and* their people to work together to improve the whole system.

Within organisations, matters that are complex and those that are simple are inescapably linked through Vital Connections. However, the nature and relationship of the simple and the complex are consistently misunderstood. Do executives in your organisation frequently remind everyone that 'it's not rocket science!'? Nurturing an organisation that is adapting and growing is both simpler than rocket science *and* more complex.

Leaders (all of us) must strive to better understand:

. . . the relation between the simple and the complex, between the universal and the individual, between the basic laws of nature and the particular.[2]

This chapter seeks to deepen our understanding of the relationship between the complex matters of people at work and the simple matter of what it means to work there.

If our approaches to the simple and complex at work are indeed upside down, it may explain:

- why leadership has been so grossly neglected
- why boardrooms focus on organisational management to the exclusion of leadership issues
- why leadership is such a desperate and critical issue in today's continuously transforming organisations.

Simplicity

In many organisations issues that should be simple are made complex. What should be simple?

- The picture of the organisation and its structure should be simple.
- The definition of 'what it means to work here' should be simple.
- Any necessary rules and the consequences of our actions should be simple.
- How we get paid for the work we contribute should be simple.
- Understanding what the organisation is trying to accomplish, and how we as individuals help the organisation to achieve its aims, should be simple.
- The description of the work we do must be simple.

These basic precepts should be considered in greater detail, and applied in every organisation.

Connections

Pictures of an organisation

If it is too difficult for each and every member of the organisation to draw a picture of the organisation telling the story of what is important to the organisation, then the message is not clear. Without a clear picture of the organisation, people wander in a directionless fog, never knowing whether their efforts help the organisation to adapt and grow. Alternatively, they fly around the organisation testing first this direction, and now that. This is rather like blindfolding someone and asking them to guess the shape of a statue by throwing marbles at it and listening to the way they bounce.* People don't need to be told which path to follow, and how to take steps that they are qualified to decide for themselves. People *do* need to understand a simply expressed destination.

A clear picture of the organisation, such as that in Figure 6.1, may be drawn that allows different business units to adapt it.

Figure 6.1 Our organisation

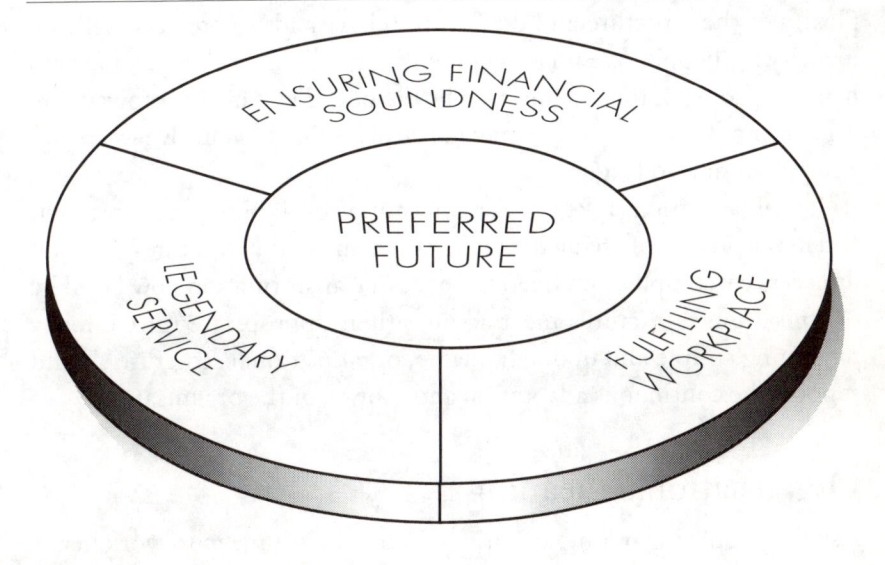

*Analogy courtesy of David Prottas, an old friend.

Each and every individual should be able to understand the picture. By keeping the picture simple, people begin to appreciate how they may contribute to the realisation of that picture. If the pictures drawn by everyone in your organisation aren't similar to one another, then the message is too complex. Does your organisation take the time to make its message simple?

How often does your organisation redo its organisational chart? Can *everyone* in the organisation tell *anyone* outside the organisation about the structure? Why is it structured that way? How does that structure support the organisation's goals?

Complex reporting lines frequently accompany such structures—titles reporting to other titles. Most of these titles are not descriptive of the work actually done. In many cases, the connections between the title and the work aren't the least bit comprehensible. In one organisation, we observed at least three layers of vice-presidents reporting up the hierarchical chain. It was impossible to understand what they did or why, or why one vice president should be more powerful than another. The complexity of the structure and descriptive chart had become a substitute identity for people. We no longer identify with our work—'my job is to help the people of the organisation be the best they can be'—now we are 'Manager of Organisational Change'. Explain that to your five-year-old, a customer or a colleague.

Organisations take the easy way out by designing structures first, and in the process of trying to manage these unwieldy structures they add unnecessary complexity. Given the pace of transformation now faced by organisations, structures must assume their appropriate function. By remaining simple and understandable, organisational structure should support the continuous adaptation and growth of the organisation.

Organisational meaning

Ask the people in your organisation: 'What does it mean to work here?' How complicated is an honest answer? Can they reach over and grab a manual from the shelf that you could glance at and, in only a minute or two, begin to understand what life is like in that organisation? Or are there manuals on top of manuals, on top of reports and recommendations? Does everyone in your company describe life there in a different fashion?

The concept of the *Survival Manual* used by Semco (Appendix D in Ricardo Semler's *Maverick*) is a great example of a simple and inspiring description of company life. It is something that may be used to lure prospective employees to the organisation, as well as a marketing tool for customers. People should be able to explain such a manual simply to a friend or family member. You know it has something going for it when employees are excited and can't wait to show it around.

Necessary rules

How many rules does your organisation have? Are they commonsense rules that apply logically to the work being done? Or has your organisation taken Fred Taylor to heart and tried to make rules about how fast anyone can breathe during reorganisation announcements? Are the rules made for an earlier set of circumstances now a nonsense in today's environment? If *everybody* doesn't know *all* of the rules of an organisation, then there are too many to know.

It is also likely that if there are too many rules to remember, the consequences of breaking those rules will be inconsistently applied. We worked in one organisation that awarded a sales professional an international trip for landing a big account. That is, until he declined the prize because he could not share it with the secretary who worked overtime to type his winning proposal. He was then informed that the next time he did that he would be sacked—sales representatives were not to go into the office and seek help! Within two months he found another job.

Financial reward

Take a look at how the people in your organisation get paid. Explore how complex pay issues have become. Yes, we consultants have been at it again, adding layers of complexity to a fairly simple concept. Pay systems have become wonderful examples of complexity run amuck. They represent valiant attempts to apply linear science to human principles.

Pay should simply be for value. If an individual contributes value to the organisation, they should benefit from that contribution. If the organisation benefits more, then the people should also. Benefits to the organisation from teams increasing its value should be shared by these teams. How the increased value is shared should be decided by the team. And that's it—no more complexity!

Why do organisations try to keep the amount of money that everyone makes a secret from everyone else? Some companies have compliance rules, which mean you can actually be sacked if you tell anyone how much you get paid. Does anyone think that pay is really a secret? It is certainly more of a mystery than it need be. How can we possibly create an atmosphere where teamwork blooms, when we create suspicion and mistrust in such an essential matter?

Pay is associated with job grades, and many organisations think Colonel Hay had all the answers. (Colonel Hay developed a system for rating the value of jobs in terms such as responsibility and reporting relationship.) He didn't even imagine the types of things that people would be doing now. Who out there can present a convincing argument for Hay Pointing 'intellectual capital'?

Perhaps most egregiously, pay is applied as a means to *use* people—to manipulate, control and humiliate. The fascinating fact is that all of the research, for in excess of 40 years, tells us that this attempt to use people *doesn't bring about outstanding performance*. In fact it does just the opposite. If there is a gun to my head I will dance, but you won't get my best. Let's take the complexity out of how we get paid and stop reinventing failed wheels.

Ben and Jerry's Ice Cream in Vermont is a 'different' company in many respects. One example of its difference is their introduction of a unique policy on employees' pay. No one—not even themselves as owners of the company—can be paid more than five times the lowest paid person in the company. Simple.

| Connections |

Organisational perspective and involvement

An understanding of what the organisation is trying to accomplish and how each individual helps the organisation to achieve it should be available to employees at every level.

Organisations have made this aspect of themselves so complex, so impersonal and so narrow that we no longer know or necessarily care what the next department is doing. When asked to do something, do people in your organisation reply 'That's not my job . . .'?

Job descriptions

The authors attended an all day session of a group of managers, who devoted part of the day to explaining to each other what their jobs were. The purpose of this was to see how they could work together better, eliminate duplication of energy and in general to impart a sense of clarity of purpose. Sounds like a good idea.

All of the participants read through job descriptions of a minimum of five pages. That's correct—*read through*. If job descriptions need to be *read*, rather than remembered, then what is being demanded of people at work is too complex or the job description is nonsensical, bearing no relation to the work. What is more, the job descriptions, as read, seemed to lack a unifying purpose (especially when they shared with many job descriptions in other organisations the line 'other duties as directed'). It became real 'tick-the-box' stuff. People will try to fulfil the complexity of the job description, rather than to find meaning at work.

Job descriptions have become too rigid in their complexity to allow for continuous adaptation and ultimately the organisation's growth. 'Job description' must be replaced with work description. A work description does not delineate the multitude of tasks to be performed—it focuses on what the organisation is attempting to achieve, and how the individual can contribute.

The role of the Critical Leader must be one of transforming or translating the unnecessarily complex into simple terms. Allow people to understand *in the simplest terms* what their work is all about and where they fit in. It is not good enough to focus on simplifying the organisational messages, although the simplification of those messages must be accomplished. Awakening Vital Connections in the organisation involves recognising and defining both the simple and the complex issues. Critical Leadership undertakes this task and attempts to understand their interaction.

Complexity

There is a tendency to pretend that how we work to get things done at work is simple. There is a longing to perfect the organisational blueprint that was espoused in the Tayloristic concept of the workplace. In many organisations complex issues are oversimplified. What is complex?

- People are complex.
- The evolution of the organisation—the way it continues to grow and adapt—is complex.
- The actual functioning of the organisation is complex.
- Understanding the means to chart the probable future of the organisation is complex.
- Learning, both as individuals and within organisations, is complex.

People are complex

People are not easy to understand. They are not ultimately controllable in any way that is ethical. People do not help an organisation adapt and grow if they are regarded as a simple aspect of its functioning, like part of a machine. Within organisations we have desperately tried to cure our ills by assuming that people can be manipulated to act only at our direction. Wrong!

People do not like complicated job descriptions that do not treat them as thinking and responsible adults. In writing such guidelines it seems that we wish to deny the humanness of our organisations, thereby forgetting that organisations are only made up of people working collaboratively. The primary purpose of an organisation is to accomplish things that we as individuals could not accomplish; it should be fundamental that organisations are built upon humanity. There is no getting around having people in the organisation. There is, therefore, no sense in trying to leave our humanness on the doorstep when we come to work.

There is a great deal of frustration within those organisations that try to deny the complexity of people. Executive directives go out along organisational communication chains and people do not change according to those messages. It is assumed that this happens because the people must not be any good—if they were, they would just do what we told them. Anyone ever try that with their children?

Sure life would be simpler for us if this system worked but the simple fact is that it won't. Let us begin to admit the complexity of the people in our organisations. It can't always be their fault if they don't understand what we are asking of them. It must be ours—the managers of the organisation. We must accept the blame, and fix the problem, by transforming how we approach the people within the organisation.

Let's celebrate and collaborate with our complexity and differences. Let's build the organisation around the greatness of the fact that we are people, we are individuals. Let's do amazing things by releasing the people from the Taylorist suppression they have been suffering all those years.

One of the great facts about people, unlike machines, is that they can adapt and grow, like plants in a garden. Given nurturing and care they accomplish amazing things. Let them help the organisation adapt and grow. Frankly, once Vital Connections begin to form within the organisation between the simple and the complex, it is too complicated and dynamic for executives to steer by themselves.

Organisational evolution

The general evolution of organisations may be followed in Weisbord's learning curve. We are now in the age of intellectual capital. It is creating new challenges for our leaders. Critical Leadership is the ability to understand the complexity of this evolution.

The Critical Leader is able to answer the questions that inevitably come from the movement through this learning curve and which stimulate it to continue towards the next necessary stage of evolution. The ability to help pilot the organisation through this uncertainty is the skill Critical Leaders acquire anew each day—to chart and make course corrections without pausing.

Daily functioning

Sometimes it is completely beyond any of us to truly understand exactly how an organisation functions because the structures and rules and policies are so complex that no mortal being could begin to approach its comprehension. Mostly, however, it is because of the often unseen way that simple and complex aspects of organisations interact.

Nevertheless, if all aspects of the organisation are moving towards the same destination, if we have that destination in common and have the organisation up and moving, then we have some possibility of obtaining our preferred future.

Different plants grow at different rates, and weeding and watering are not necessarily needed uniformly within the garden. The gardener must know when to do the things necessary and must always be watchful for where care and assistance are required.

Charting the probable future

The preferred future, as a destination, is only achieved through 'approximate equations', ones that will *probably* achieve the next milestone on the journey. There is no guarantee that the seeds you sow now will ever germinate, or that the garden will look *exactly* as planned. By establishing or reviving the links between your Vital Connections, the probability of arriving at the journey's destination is enhanced. Through the continuous expansion of Vital Connections the pace of the journey accelerates.

Too often organisations place barriers in their own way, inhibiting instant course corrections as the turbulent environment shifts and dances. It is silly to build a brick wall around your garden and omit the door.

Organisational restructuring of the recent past has been like hit squads coming in after a replanting and building a wall so strong and tall that the organisation is not able to expand without destroying that wall. The organisation is not able to adapt to new conditions because of the imposed confinements. The people of the organisation are not able to receive the continuous care they need. Restructuring assumed that there was a straight path towards the preferred goals. The restructuring has also assumed that there is a desired status quo. Reorganisations assumed that there will be no earthquakes as the organisation travels that path. They have not accounted for environmental changes and shocks, where only the fast and flexible are able to adapt to any situation to continue to grow.

It is not the scientist, engineer or accountant we need to pilot the organisation towards its preferred future. The Critical Leader must combine the knowledge of systems thinker, the skill of the orchestral conductor, the love of the gardener and the wit of the hunted animal.

Organisational learning

Do the people in your organisation learn? Do they learn every day? If they do, does your organisation learn? Continuously? From everyone? This is a hard one. It is also one that cannot (currently) be measured or quantified. We are not referring to training or passing tests or evaluating skill levels within the organisation. Adapting and growing only takes place when the organisation is able to *learn*. It must know *how* to learn. That is the one important element—not what it has learned. It must also know how to transfer the knowledge quickly through the organisation. People must continuously share all of their knowledge and learn in an almost morphogenic fashion.

Critical Leaders understand that everything we know about running organisations today, all of the skills, methods, theories and structure, will be obsolete tomorrow. Critical Leaders look for the 'next place'. They do not oversimplify the complexity of organisational learning.

How many people really understand what Peter Senge means when he describes the learning organisation?[3] The idea seems to elude most organisational leaders. Is it the complexity of an interactive system that has us shying away from the concept of organisational learning? In the quest to simplify the wrong aspects of organisations, we shut out that which is complex but vital.

Connecting

The Critical Leader's work must be dedicated to defining the simple and complex. And then making the appropriate connections. A summary of the simple and the complex in organisations is given in Table 6.1.

The simple aspects of organisational design are defining where the garden is to be planted, deciding the types of flowers desired, determining how rich the soil should be, the pattern the plants will grow in . . .

Table 6.1 The simple and the complex

Should be simple:	The complex:
Organisational picture/structure	People
What it means to work here	Organisational evolution
Rules	Daily functioning
Pay for value	Charting the probable future
Goals and how we contribute	Organisational learning
Job descriptions	

Connections

The complex aspects of organisational design are the nurturing and caring part of growing the garden—the complexity of each individual plant, and the complexity of their relationship to an ever-changing environment. Plants may be coaxed and watered, but they cannot be forced.

Interaction

Simple things have complex effects. The complex affects the simple. They must be working in tandem along the webs of interconnectivity that allow an organisation to function and drive it towards its preferred future. The slightest adjustment in one creates an impact in the other. This phenomenon is described by Murray Gell-Mann:

There remains the widespread phenomenon of chaos, in which the outcome of a dynamical process is so sensitive to initial conditions that a minuscule change in the situation at the beginning of the process results in a large difference at the end.[4]

There is nothing that occurs within an organisation that does not affect everything else, just like an ecosystem. We must first understand what should be simple or complex, and then begin to understand the effects of one on the other. We must also be prepared for actions and deeds with consequences far greater than first intended or expected.

There is absolutely no separating the simple from the complex. How we approach one, define the borders of the garden, adding water to the garden affects the health and well-being of the plants that are flourishing. People become disoriented within their organisation when we get the simple and complex upside down. When we try to either separate the simple from the complex or attempt to deny the reality of complexity we create blockages to our organisational journey.

Roses and Rust

If we confuse or misunderstand the simple and the complex, what would the impact on the organisation's goals be? We worked with one organisation that had over 40 instruction manuals (which stacked up to 1.8 metres). It was not possible for the people in the organisation to hear the messages from the CEO or the customers about improving customer service, as no one was prepared to step around the rule books. Similarly, the first step towards success at Semco (Ricardo Semler's company) was to rip up the rule books.

The organisation that has mistaken the things that are properly simple for those things that are really complex has created the need for universal leadership within the organisation. That is, leadership by everyone within the organisation in order to drive the organisation forward and reorient the organisation's priorities. The implications of turning the current approach to the simple and the complex on its head is huge—it means most current managers needs to rethink their purpose. This is because:

- There are fewer things to manage.
- Energy must be shifted from the management of things.
- Energy must be shifted into the understanding and leadership of complexity.
- Layers within organisations which existed in order to supervise (control the formerly complex rules and structures) will disappear.
- The current organisational intellect will be stretched to breaking.
- Leaders will emerge with an understanding of the complex aspects of organisations made of people, and find their role is one of helping.

The organisation must be built around its people and the core competencies* they are able to bring to their environment, not around processes and technology and missions. This demands cognisance of complexity. Leaders must understand the interconnectivity of all the relationships

---

* We refer the reader to our discussion on core competencies in Chapter 9.

within an organisation, and in so doing they will define the simplicity and complexity of the organisation and its functions.

Through facilitating these connections, the pathway towards the organisation's preferred future opens and begins to clear. The probable attainment of that future increases. Critical Leaders must reconceptualise their organisation--in a fundamentally different way from the existing concepts of re-engineering and restructuring and reorganising. Critical Leaders conceptualise their organisation as a complex adaptive system:

The common feature of all these processes is that in each one a complex adaptive system acquires information about its environment and its own interaction with that environment, identifying regularities in that information, condensing those regularities into a kind of 'schema' or model, and acting in the real world on the basis of that schema.[5]

In order to allow the organisation to follow its schema or model we must right the orientation of the system. This allows for the application of the Vital Connections of the organisation to be clearly observed for what they are. It involves the redefining of those things which should be simple, and currently are not.

Critical Leaders must appreciate that organisations have been built around concepts which are indeed upside down. They must be critical of our tendency to spend so much of our time on process and technology, and so little trying to understand interactions between the people of the organisation.

The Vital Connections of the organisation must be understood as simple or complex, and they must be appropriately enabled and supported.

Discovery

Connections
How are the following elements treated in your organisation?

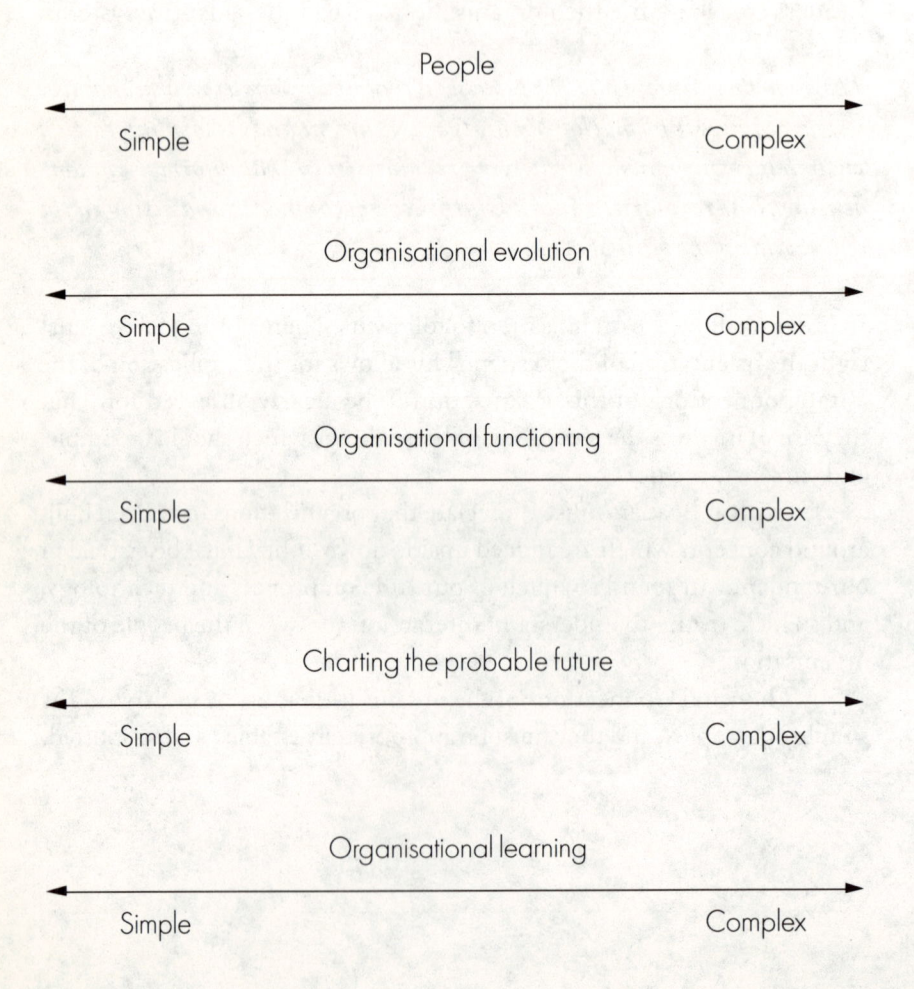

People

Simple ←————————————————————→ Complex

Organisational evolution

Simple ←————————————————————→ Complex

Organisational functioning

Simple ←————————————————————→ Complex

Charting the probable future

Simple ←————————————————————→ Complex

Organisational learning

Simple ←————————————————————→ Complex

| Connections |

Organisational picture

Simple ←——————————————————————→ Complex

Organisational structure

Simple ←——————————————————————→ Complex

What it means to work here

Simple ←——————————————————————→ Complex

Rules

Simple ←——————————————————————→ Complex

Pay for value

Simple ←——————————————————————→ Complex

Goals and how we each contribute

Simple ←——————————————————————→ Complex

Job descriptions

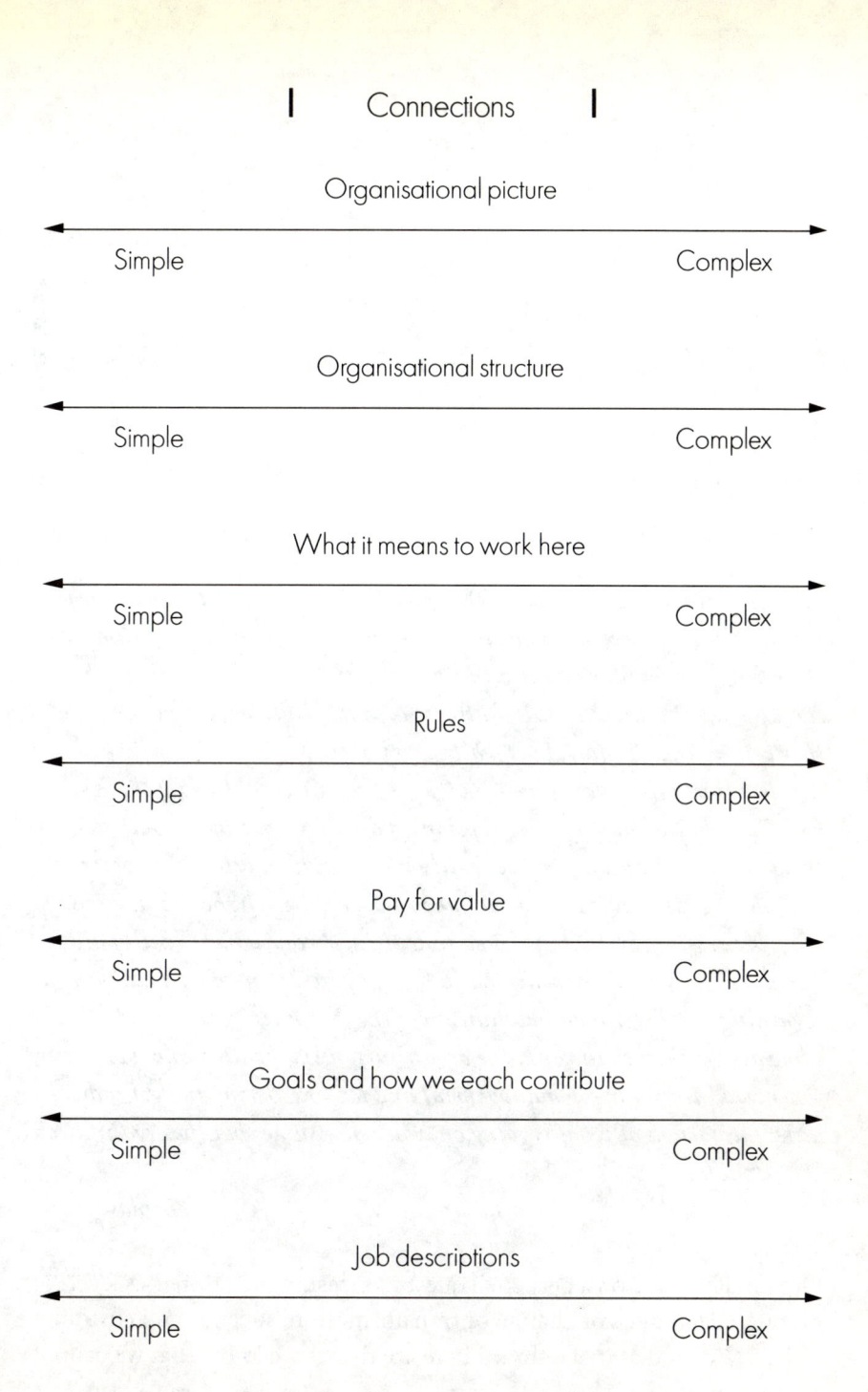

Simple ←——————————————————————→ Complex

7.
Knowing

... the perceptions of people, especially top management, present a real problem in interpreting what is and is not. Managers often assume that their perceptions of the world, and especially of their own operations, carry a special load of credibility. And after years of consulting, I'm not sure why they believe that. In fact, I get a bit weary of saying to managers who have problems with their departments or with their careers, 'I know that's what you think, but what are the perceptions of others?' That they should concern themselves with how others see reality is a foreign and threatening concept to them ... Managers often become so involved with themselves, so self-absorbed, that they are convinced that their perceptions of reality are the true ones ... My experience is that when the perceptions of top management regarding the direction and condition of the corporation are essentially the same as those lower in rank, the organisation is a healthy one. However, when you interview top management and lower echelons and get radically different notions of what is going on, you can assume that the organisation is in trouble.

Thomas Quick[1]

Organisations are on a perpetual quest to measure such things as levels of morale, acceptance of change or transformation, success, and customer satisfaction or dissatisfaction. There are things we know that we cannot prove, and there are a thousand things that we can prove that aren't worth knowing. And in between the two, there are opportunities for action and inaction. How an organisation *knows* is a critical issue during transformational quakes. Anyone who claims to know The Answer to the question of organisational change is a fool or worse.

Knowing is an important topic for organisations to continually explore. Organisations frequently buy solutions from external consultants because they presume that consultants know something the organisation does not.

There are no recipes or formulae, no checklists or advice that describe 'reality'. There is only what we create through our engagement with others and with events. Nothing really transfers, everything is always new and different and unique to each of us.[2]

Organisations believe that evaluations can measure the pay-offs that result from specific interventions. The established methods of knowing therefore continue to be applied unchallenged. However, Imparato and Harari recount the words of Nobel laureate Fredrich Hayek who argued that '. . . economists must understand that the complex phenomena of the market will hardly ever be fully known or measurable . . .'[3] Organisations must accept that effective methods of transformation are as unquantifiable and unpredictable as the markets.

Unbounded systems thinking

There is a wonderful work by Mitroff and Linstone titled *The Unbounded Mind: Breaking the Chains of Traditional Business Thinking*. It is one of the works that strongly promote the use of a *whole systems approach to knowing*. This approach argues that we must clearly understand the interconnectedness of all things within a business in order to gauge the probable results of any of our actions. The outcomes of the transformational quakes of an organisation cannot be known totally, but—if we understand the intricacies of the organisation—actions may be made congruently with the desired outcomes. Too often, transformations are thought of in a simplistic fashion, focusing internally on processes. They frequently ignore the truly complex plotting of likely reactions from the huge number of people surrounding the transformation. This includes the workforce, suppliers, customers and shareholders. Once that many people are involved or affected by the transformation the complexity of the outcomes is impossible to completely grasp.

Mitroff and Linstone discuss five ways of knowing:

- *agreement*, which relies on common observations to define and structure problems
- *analysis*, which creates scientific models and observes as the models are tested
- *multiple realities*, which states that many models and observations are more likely to define truth than one model
- *conflict*, which looks at the confrontation of opposites—this is the adversarial method that many countries apply to establishing guilt or innocence in the courtroom
- *unbounded systems thinking*, which is based on the premise that 'everything interacts with everything'.

All these methods provide information and some knowledge. The knowledge provided by the first four methods is flawed in some sense or another. They each have benefits, but fail to look at the whole and most assume a static status quo.

The approach to knowing which Mitroff and Linstone have adopted, unbounded systems thinking (UST), draws on the works of Edgar Singer who did much early work in the field of systems thinking. In introducing UST they employ three perspectives: the technical perspective (T); the organisational or societal perspective (O); and the personal or individual perspective (P). The primary advantage of UST over the other four methods of thinking is that the O and P perspectives are introduced. The technical perspective has long been the sole focus—the linear approach. The O and P perspectives introduced here bring the 'people aspects' of any problem right to the foreground. As Mitroff and Linstone state:

> ... *the difference in perspectives forces us to distinguish how we are looking from what we are looking at. Each incorporates distinct sets of underlying assumptions and values.*[4]

Additionally, their research enables them to state:

> *Effective organisations are usually characterised by a strong congruence between the O perspective and their members' P perspective.*[5]

Work in systems thinking and its applications has been made even more accessible to organisations by people like Marvin Weisbord, who applies it in *Productive Workplaces* and *Discovering Common Ground*.

Weisbord challenges us to view our organisations as though we were viewing everything we see through a movie camera. The camera may be moved around, shifted to look at things from all different angles. He has presented organisations with a useful tool called the All-Purpose Viewfinder. This viewfinder asks us to look at our organisations from at least six different angles.

We have modified the Viewfinder to enable decisions to take into account their impact on the future (see Figure 7.1). The modification is required if the organisation is going to be capable of transformation or reinvention. How many people in your organisation explore each issue from at least six perspectives? How many people actively employ a systems approach to understanding the impacts of any action on achieving the organisation's preferred future. Try encouraging the application of this 'all-purpose viewfinder' in meetings and gatherings, see if participants will go along, and then see how rapidly your organisation benefits from systems thinking.

Figure 7.1 All-Purpose Viewfinder

	Inside picture	Outside picture	Preferred future
Economics $	Costs + or -	N/A	Where will our margins come from?
	N/A	Revenue + or -	Where will our revenue come from?
Technology and systems	Do systems work as intended?	N/A	What channels will we need to reach customers in the future?
	N/A	Are products and systems being improved?	What innovations may be appropriate for us?
People	How do our people feel about working here? What skills and capabilities make us unique today?	N/A	What should we do to ensure that our people are the best they can be and that we offer unique skills and capabilities?
	N/A	How do our customers feel about buying here?	Which customers will we be serving in the future?

Source: Adapted from Marvin Weisbord's All-Purpose Viewfinder in Marvin R. Weisbord (1987) *Productive Workplaces: Organizing and Managing for Dignity, Meaning and Community*, San Francisco: Jossey-Bass, p. 272.

Knowing

Tony Richardson and Jock Macneish[6] poke fun at how we view organisations and their accessible work reminds us that we need to look at the whole system to understand an organisation. It was Richardson and Macneish who introduced us to the view of the organisation as a big jelly (or for the Yank writing here, a jello mold). The picture communicates instantly and powerfully what is meant by a systems approach. Touch any part of the jelly, even a little, and the whole thing moves.

How do you know?

Currently, organisations do not challenge *how* they know. This is problematic for two primary reasons:

1. Knowledge is one of the key tools of leadership during organisational quakes. Processes are reinvented, values redefined, people restructured and customer expectations reassessed—yet we *know*, or measure, all these things using methods from the past. Charles Handy tells us, in *Understanding Organizations*, that it is important to know when to discard past learning. Things learned in the past may be totally inappropriate to anything at all in the future. The appropriateness of using past methodologies of knowing and measuring must be challenged.
2. Decisions are made (or evaded) based on these inappropriate 'methods of knowing'. If the critical decisions taken daily based on erroneous knowledge were revealed, it would frighten us so much that all actions would be questionable. This fear may benefit the organisation, creating the wake-up call desperately needed within the ranks of organisations facing profound change. The wake-up call is required simply because so many people suffer because of illconceived ideas about what creates change.

The difficulties of driving transformation are greatly compounded by inappropriately skilled managers interpreting the results of inadequate methods of 'knowing' about the organisation. At some point we need to truly understand what Margaret Wheatley means when she says that we must learn to be trusting '. . . in the unfolding dance of order'. We must now understand concepts of order from a completely different perspective. Managers often confuse order with sequential, linear and controlled actions. If things don't appear orderly we seek to impose a familiar order to achieve certainty. However, if that certainty is based on information gathered inappropriately, and we apply a step-by-step approach to action, we have the formula for disaster. Perhaps it is really an inability to understand things from multiple or holistic perspectives that explains why transforming an organisation is such a difficult task, and why it so seldom succeeds.

Organisational paradox

'What gets measured gets done! By measuring something we can control human behaviour.' This seems to be something akin to tribal folklore within organisations. It also implies that things which we really can't measure (such as how much of someone's mind and heart they bring to the tasks at work) won't get done or don't matter within the workplace. The conclusion might well be that we don't need creativity or desire within the workforce. But who believes that an organisation can transform itself, becoming adaptable in order to compete in the future, without the creativity and desire of the people working there?

The more something an adult does is monitored, the less the desire to do the task! Alfie Kohn, in *Punished by Rewards*, cites abundant evidence showing that the more you look over the shoulder of an adult, the less desirable the task becomes.

The more you measure something, the more people are prone to provide you with the answers they believe that you want. Dr John Evans, of Cultural Imprint, observes in his work that the more people are asked, particularly in stressful environments, the more likely they are to try and guess what answers are the ones that keep the organisation at bay.

Knowing

During organisational transformation, traditional methods of knowing how the organisation is performing need to be enhanced by applications of the Viewfinder, gaining the shared perceptions of the people, intuition, common sense and feelings. When you walk into a workplace, does it overflow with excitement for the task at hand or does it seem mundane and run down? What CEO steering a company through the stress of a transformation actually believes everyone when they say that 'Things are right' or 'There are no problems' or 'Don't worry, we'll get it done'?

This *may* mean everything is fine but it probably means that people are not willing to discuss their trauma. The care of the people needs to play a large role in our approach to understanding whether or not the people are healthy and things are getting done.

Unfortunately, this means we need to rekindle our ability to trust in others—even if this means allowing for occasional disappointments on the journey.

Exploring critical understanding

The path towards knowing begins with an exploration of the organisation. What are the critical things we need to know about our organisation? Why are these things critical? How shall we go about understanding these things?

Critical questions could include:

- Are we making money so that we can competitively stay in business?
- Are we providing our customers with the service expected? (Are they experiencing exceptional 'moments of truth'?)
- Do the people who work here understand the business we are in, and how they positively contribute to the success of that business every day? (What does it mean to work here?)

- Is there a clearly communicated picture of the purpose of the organisation? Is there a clearly communicated preferred future of the organisation?

We need to explore what makes us really feel that we know. We must challenge past methods of knowing. These include traditional surveys, open forums for discussion of problems, short-term results of anything, such as sales closed or financial improvements or reports. It includes finding answers that represent certainty.

Our hope is to leave you with our own thoughts on 'knowing', some interesting perspectives from other thinkers and an application or two for your use. We hope this encourages your quest for knowledge to expedite your organisational transformation.

Dead cats and soufflés

People who actually understand things like quantum physics pose an interesting question concerning measurement. The quantum world that is gradually becoming known to us 'non-scientists' seems to tell us that we must learn to appreciate the *probable outcomes* of actions and events. Before we can measure, we must appreciate that only probabilities exist. It also tells us that the act of measurement itself influences the outcome.

The theory of 'Schroedinger's Cat'[7] suggests that the act of measuring influences the outcome of some processes. These outcomes may not be the same outcomes had we not measured the process or object. The hypothetical situation (over-simplified) is that within a box is a cat and some poison and some food. Until the box is opened the cat is neither alive nor dead. Or, the cat is both. It is only the act of opening the box, or the act of observation, which decides the fate of the cat. This argument was used to describe the dilemma of observation of electrons, which until measured are both particles and waves, but when observed may only be one or the other. John Gribbin states that 'common sense has already been tested as a guide to quantum reality and been found wanting'.

This theory suggests to us that organisations cease seeking The Answer and begin to explore multiple potentials. Margaret Wheatley explains this issue and beautifully relates it to how it may be applied by organisations. She suggests that we need to be aware of all the possibilities and potentials instead of striving for the single objective 'truth'. The act of measuring or passing judgment in our quest for this single answer denies us the opportunity to explore and appreciate possibilities. Long-held expectations and previous experience often corrupt our 'objective judgment'.

We find these concepts fascinating, and believe that they hold fundamental truths for Critical Leadership within transforming organisations. However, in our attempt to truly understand the physics and apply this wisdom to benefit organisations, to build an understanding of *indeterminate futures*, we find it easier to talk about it in terms of soufflés. Indeterminate futures are the only certainty of organisational quakes.

Now, making a soufflé is fraught with danger. (We must assume this from hearsay and TV sitcoms, since neither of us has ever actually been involved in the making of a soufflé.) It appears as though one should get the ingredients, mix it up, set the oven just right and place it to bake. Now for the central dilemma. Imagine that the oven in which the soufflé is baking does not have a glass door—so you can't see it. How do you know that it is baking all right? You may want to peek, but you know that if you do it will probably result in the soufflé's collapse—disaster! So how might you *know* how it's doing?

You simply can't, and at this point all the work and measurement in the world does not help. You simply must trust that it feels right. If you believe it does not, then certainly, you should open the oven, and prepare to begin again.

Sometimes knowing is as simple as that—it seems to have been constructed all right, it smells good, and it's not the right time to ask for a result. But what trust and confidence you need to have to approach knowing within your organisation that way!

When your curiosity demands to know something about the business results of your organisation, particularly during organisational quakes, you should pause and think deeply about whether it is the right time to open the door and find out.

False truths and contempt

Kriegel and Patler (*If It Ain't Broke—Break It*) refer to the negative fear cycles we inadvertently move through in times of high stress.

It seems natural for us to focus on the negative, to the exclusion of the positive. But because we have not factored in positive experiences, our assessment isn't accurate.[8]

A focus on these 'false truths' can warp the way you see your organisation, and can make the need for corrective or evasive action appear so desperate that dangerous linear approaches may be adopted. Much organisational pain created is based upon false truths.

Remembering that organisational quakes are times of high stress, what are the things that your organisation dwells on? Is your organisation focused on making balanced assessments?

How much time do you spend on false truths—looking at just the negative side of the organisational picture? Imagine yourself walking into the workplace, whether it be a factory or distribution centre or branch office. Think about what you first look for. Do you seek out what is going really well and applaud those responsible, or do you seek the things that may not be up to your expectations?

David used to run around the world teaching seminars on a variety of financial topics. Even on those occasions where he was extremely successful in communicating with the participants, and we clearly made progress up the knowledge hill, he would be depressed for hours over one bad score or negative comment about his efforts, to the exclusion of all positive comments.

Think about how you approach issues in your personal life with friends or families. If your child returns home with fabulous results on a science test, do you ask about that one question they got wrong? There is ample psychological evidence around to demonstrate the powerfully negative effects of this approach. It breeds a fear of failure. This is not an environment in which people feel safe enough to be the best they can be.

Do leaders and managers in your organisation continuously point out the negatives in the name of continuous improvement or constructive criticism? (Now there's an oxymoron for you.) Does the organisation quickly make it apparent that the reason for knowing and measuring is so that the negatives can be found out and corrected?

It seems impossible for the people of the organisation to ever know if they are making progress if all that are measured are mistakes. In such an environment self-esteem and confidence cannot last long. In your organisation do people know that they do good work only when they are not belittled?

Organisations which approach knowing in this manner are taking the easy way out. They limit the perspective of what is happening and drive simplistic solutions, such as do this or else. This is similar to the participants in brainstorming sessions who trash all ideas proposed. It is easy to put down any idea, it is hard to find one and make it work. Does your organisation look for the satisfaction of its customers and try to exceed that, or does it measure dissatisfaction levels and look at problem solving? Which organisation do you believe is focused on the future? Focus on growing a robust garden, rather than hammering any imperfections into shape.

Thoughts on measurements and knowledge...

Organisations must perform and be fit or they will not survive. It is imperative to contribute value and to make money. Time spent chasing false truths does not contribute any particular value either to the organisation or to its customers. If the organisation is only focused on developing actions based on false truths, it can never plot a path to its preferred future. Will that approach within an organisation allow for the knowledge of the probable outcomes from any and all actions undertaken?

Many organisations appear to be weak in their approach to the 'sales and service' aspect of a prosperous business. Mediocrity may be continuously achieved, but the sales and service focus never takes off in a big way. Why? While there may be myriad reasons, blame is frequently focused on the sales force. They 'lack focus', or 'commitment'. Management then undertakes corrective behavioural actions. To focus the sales force and gain commitment, new and better reward and incentive systems are put in place. This example, which we believe to be quite common, reveals misunderstanding in several areas:

- the *focus* does not explore the whole system, internally and externally
- the *solution* to the problem typically does not look at the whole system, internally and externally.

Organisations often devise solutions aimed at correcting the behaviours of the workforce. These actions just as frequently fracture the workforce. This is because they do not involve the whole system in the 'corrective' process.

The linear approach to knowing both what is going on in a transforming organisation (and to knowing what the potential impact of any and all actions will be) is simply inadequate for the degree and pace of the quakes occurring. The linear approaches adopted run parallel to the false truths accepted.

We *all* need to challenge the way things are done *continuously*. Kouzes and Posner's extensive research tells us that one of the five leadership practices followers expect is 'challenging the process'. This becomes critical for leaders during transformational quakes. Challenge must be a continuous process, and it must incorporate a challenge to 'how we know'. Do we challenge the measurement systems within our organisations? Do we create dramatic, quantum changes—but then use knowledge systems from the distant past? We must find the skills in our organisation to apply systems thinking by each and every member and to apply it to each and every issue. We must explore the knowledge we might steal from science or other disciplines for measuring and knowing.

Knowledge must now be viewed in terms of possible rather than definitive answers. All possibilities should then be plotted in terms of their potential outcomes. Failure to approach knowledge in this fashion will lead to an ultimate lack of credibility for the leaders of the organisation.

Soufflé recipes . . .

Critical Leadership is all about helping the people within the organisation to be the best they can be. They, in turn, will assist the organisation to adapt and grow. Critical Leaders continuously question how the organisation is doing on its transformational journey. To reinforce the direction of the journey, the leader's questions must focus on the multiple possible paths which lead towards the organisation's preferred future. They must develop the skills required to understand the reactions of people, particularly in times of stress. Their search for knowledge must always acknowledge that there is no one right answer. Questioning, always from many viewpoints, must be used as a method to continuously close the gap of perception which is the ultimate block to the successful transformation of an organisation on the path to adaptability.

Understanding mutually preferred futures

Do you and the people you work with have a mutual perception of a preferred future? How do you *really know* if this perception is shared? One recipe for beginning to understand mutual perceptions of the organisation can be performed in less than 20 minutes with a group. The group can use the information gathered to keep or get them mutually focused over a long period of time.

All you need are crayons and flip-chart paper. It is important to limit the time, and to display the results, discussing them when anyone wants. It is a 'limited' adaptation of future searches, but one which seems to fit the tight time frames of organisations in the midst of organisational quakes—who don't have the two or three days typically required to perform traditional searches.

Here's what you do. Give everyone a sheet of paper and a packet of crayons. Ask everyone to draw three pictures on the paper so that they will all show when the paper is hung on the wall. The first picture should be a representation of how they feel work was for them in the past. This may be a picture of the organisation, their area or their job. The second picture should be a representation of how they feel about the workplace now—what the job is like, how they feel when they come to work. The third and final picture should be of what they ideally would like the preferred future to be about.

We are continually amazed at the commonality that is expressed by groups when they draw their preferred futures. After the drawings are done, you can play Mussorgsky's *Pictures at an Exhibition* and display the pictures either on the floor or up on the wall. Anyone is allowed to ask anyone else about their picture. Everyone should then be involved with bringing out the common themes of the past, present and future. The question that must then be dealt with as a group going forward is, 'If we have this commonality, what is stopping us from achieving the mutual preferred future?' This simple exercise lets a group acquire a mutual picture of the future and specific knowledge of what it would take to achieve that future. The real trick is to keep the group focused on this future and overcoming the obstacles they face.

Important daily tasks

Do you and your people and colleagues collectively understand the daily tasks that must be accomplished in order to bring about organisational transformation? It doesn't matter whether this change is aimed towards an adaptive integrated organisation or to transforming the culture to a more customer focused approach. It is actually incredible to see that while we may see the same potential future, our individual ideas on how to get there differ so radically. It is important to bring the picture of the preferred future and the various methods of getting there together.

This is not meant to imply that the methods must be prescriptive or exactly the same for everyone, but we believe that methods must be compatible with the direction. This can quicken the pace of the transformation dramatically.

First, have all the people in your group list the ten most important tasks which they believe they should do every day in order to bring about the preferred future. Have them list the tasks in the priority order they would give them.*

Next, using the task lists, have everyone conduct an interview with someone else in the group. The intention of this meeting is to find mutual agreement on those tasks, and on their relative priority. Continue this process until the entire group has interviewed each other. Now list the tasks and discuss how close you all are to a mutual perception of what must be done. Finally, align this to the preferred future which the group has drawn.

The benefits of this approach (and the soufflé recipe) are several:

- they can be done over an extended period of time—there is no need to accomplish everything at one meeting or sitting
- they involve the whole group, which may be, for example, two functional areas which need to work together, or the sales force and the customer
- they can be performed in the workplace during work
- they create mutual understanding which can extend into maintaining the health of the organisation through its Vital Connections.

---

*This technique was first presented to us by Dr John Evans, Cultural Imprint.

The only 'truth' that can exist within an organisation is one of mutual knowledge and shared perceptions. The absence of a shared truth or mutual knowledge is commonplace, and a guarantee of an unhealthy organisation.

The health of the organisation is the health of its internal Vital Connections. Critical Leaders will promote this health by working with the people to establish an understanding of what it takes to bring about organisational transformation. They will maintain the health by making communication a consuming part of their work.

Establishing, checking and maintaining shared perceptions is the organisation's way of knowing. And the organisation as a garden has one truth—putting energy into the people and Vital Connections provides the greatest opportunity for superior performance.

A scenario

The manager of a country bank branch had attended, over a 12 month period, sales training programs which were a part of the bank's intention to become a 'sales' culture. There had also been road shows and corporate propaganda about the need to increase sales.

There had been no improvement in the branch's sales over this period. However, within one month of attending a five day residential management development program focused on team-building skills, her branch gained a new corporate account worth over $1 million.

This manager's organisation wants to know the reason for the improvement so that it can become more efficient. In the future it will only repeat what it knows will work.

- Was the seed planted by the sales training?
- Did the manager discover some new means of focusing the team after the management program?

- Did the customer join the bank because it was dissatisfied with its former bank? (The current bank had contributed little to establishing the connection.)
- Did the telling staff make the difference? (The opening of the new account had nothing to do with the manager.)
- Did the corporate messages spark the staff to work differently?

An equation for determining the exact answer would have too many variables to be useful, or even possible.

The only truth here would be whatever the people inside and outside the branch agreed on. Any 'corporate evaluation program' could not capture the truth. It may measure at the wrong time—measuring the day before the account opened, it would not be there; the week after, and it may have gone again. It may ask the wrong questions or not enough questions, and it may ask the wrong people.

It may also be measuring the wrong things:

- Was the account worth getting? Is it profitable to the bank? Is it too expensive to maintain?
- Is the branch retaining customers? For every customer it gets, does it lose another customer?
- What was the nature of the competitor business, the bank that lost the account?

Endeavours to establish the cause and effect between initiatives and results belong to the mindset of those who see the organisation operating as a machine.

The scenario revisited

All of the above holds true but the organisation appreciates that a number of Vital Connections contributed to the performance. The organisation recognises that a lot of energy needs to be contributed to many Vital Connections to make the whole thing work.

The organisation does not waste its time and energy on a quest for proof because it knows that energy that goes into one part of the organisation as a garden helps the whole to flourish.

The organisation succeeds because Critical Leaders 'manage by tinkering"—putting energy into the people and the Vital Connections. Each member of staff continues to participate in learning programs, some of which are on selling and service; the manager coaches each of her people and meets with each of them fortnightly—there is a daily kick-off meeting and a monthly staff meeting.

The manager catches people doing something right, and continues to be visible to both her people and her customers.

The regional manger phones each week to discuss performance and visits each month. She writes a letter every time she notes a special effort or achievement.

The scenario as it sometimes occurs

No one does anything until they can prove what will pay-off. Once again, this is the organisation as a machine—things go round and round but without energy or progress.

---

* We owe the idea of 'managing by tinkering' to Margaret Wheatley, who made this observation at the 1994 ASTD Annual Conference.

Discovery

Knowing

The machine	*The garden*
Evaluations measure pay-offfs from specific interventions	Effective methods of transformation are complex and unquantifiable
Analysis, multiple realities, agreement, conflict are the best ways of knowing	Systems thinking is the best means of understanding
The technical or management is the appropriate perspective	People in the organisation explore issues from up to six perspectives
Measurement of function and process ensures their best performance	Trust and excitement are better guarantees of high performance
The organisation seeks definite answers from systems of measurement	The organisation recognises multiple potentials; challenge is continuous
Management constantly watches for mistakes or unmet expectations	Leaders seek outstanding performance and applaud those responsible

8.
Deciding

[Douglas McGregor, the originator of Theory X and Theory Y] ... decided on graduate training in psychology, choosing his school by tossing a coin. When it came up Stanford (heads), he knew from his reaction that Harvard (tails) was where he really wanted to go. Most tough decisions, he told his friends, could be made that way; the heart's desire emerged the moment the coin landed.[1]

Organisational quakes are predictable in neither their timing nor their consequences. They cannot be met or anticipated with the linear approach to decision-making or problem-solving that is so frequently taught to managers.

As we discussed in Chapter 7, organisations and their environment are far too complex for easy answers and simple logic. The future is beyond our knowing and our current approach to making decisions, or not making decisions, can be a liability.

The do-or-die challenge for Critical Leaders is to help their organisations to become adaptive. All else—the ability to grow, the need to help people to be their best, the contribution to promoting community, dignity, respect and kindness at work—follows from this. Adaptive cultures are the result of decisions that are made with courage, without the restrictive weight of past history and with a trust in the unfolding order of things.

Deciding

There are very few practices from the past that can be invoked to remove the responsibility of decision-making. Applying the 'best practices' of others is a shallow response if they are applied in the hope of assuring success. While they may work in the improvement of processes, they will never have The Answer for the Vital Connections, the people, the customers and the culture that are unique to each organisation.

Decisions have to be made about your organisation's customers and its people. Each 'lesson' from elsewhere has to be reviewed in the light of the energies that operate through the Vital Connections that make your organisation.

Adopting 'best practices' from other organisations may provide the illusion that an organisation is changing. This approach, however, is another example of treating the organisation as a machine—change a few component parts or add another product/service and the machine will have more appeal to customers or operate more efficiently and effectively.

This approach does not satisfy the need for an organisation to become adaptive. It represents a process of modifying the status quo rather than the reinvention or renewal of the organisation that is now required.

An adaptive organisation contains many fields of energy that enable it to internally generate a response to its environment. People, skills and practices must be able to emerge as they are required. The internal patterns of the organisation must be able to constantly shift in response to the environment. Creating and maintaining an adaptive organisation that is alive to its environment requires decisions. Some can be made by teams, others will require the Critical Leader to be self-reliant and make them without the support or consent of the people.

The need to be self-reliant should not be confused with being an autocratic leader. It must be recognised that some decisions cannot and should not be made by the team.[2] IBM at one time was so dedicated to consensus decision-making that, while its team was unable to decide whether to purchase MS-DOS for a relative pittance, Microsoft came in and made a world-changing decision. The phenomenon of dumb groups that are comprised of bright individual members is known to us all.

An uncertain age

Economists routinely disagree about the correct interpretation of economic events in their prescriptions for a brighter economic future. Educationalists disagree about the best way of educating our children. Nutritionists and other health professionals disagree about the components of a healthy diet. In the face of all this disagreement, the ordinary citizen feels increasingly uneasy about his or her own ability to make sensible decisions.[3]

The organisation as a machine places great value on making the 'right' decisions. It will spend an enormous amount of time and energy gathering data or information to help it make decisions. It may even be driven by the best of intentions, such as improving customer service, but it will never know if its surveys and measurements have told it the right story or provided the correct information.

Such organisations are often characterised by indecisiveness, as managers are not capable of taking the decision-making risks that are inherent in unpredictable times. Tom Peters reports a study of the decision-making of microcomputer firms that were able to produce results in less than a third of the time of their competitors. He notes that 'Slow deciders were stymied by conflict. They [wait for consensus and delay] in hopes that the uncertainty will magically become certain.'[4]

The uncertainty will never become certain. There are only probabilities and risks. What we have come to know as 'chaos' brings turbulence, magic and opportunities but its certainties and order only emerge with hindsight. Indecisiveness can weaken the ability of an organisation to respond to a turbulent environment by depleting the energy of people and damaging internal Vital Connections. External Vital Connections are also damaged as organisations become increasingly unresponsive to their environment by their inability to deliver quickly on opportunities that are only there for a fleeting moment.

Sometimes activity is mistaken for decisiveness. Managers desire both routine and time. Instead of making decisions they will start projects and committees, write memos, develop proposals, seek the opinions of others. A comparative study of high and average performers reported that average performers dealt in information.[5] For them 'taking the initiative' meant writing a memo about a problem. High performers defined 'taking the initiative' as fixing the problem.

In the machine organisation even decisiveness, which has been heralded as a value, will not result in decisions that are good for the organisation in the long term. This is because such decisions fail to work with the Vital Connections within the organisation. They are often made with a focus on the bottom line rather than the potential that is offered by an interaction with the environment and the uncertain future. If Vital Connections are weakened or hurt by decisions, there will inevitably be an effect on performance. Managers know this—as they often speak in terms of the trade-off involved in certain decisions.

In these organisations decisions perceived as poor can be punished. The chairman of a major Australian mining company announced at the 1994 annual general meeting that, after the dismissal of the last CEO, executives were now managing on the POGO principle—Perform Or Get Out. (This occurred after a poor bottom line that year—was the potential of the CEO's decisions for the future considered?) The stakes are high for people in the machine organisation. If their decisions are not perceived to be good they can be demoted, reprimanded, have their pay reduced or be retrenched.

Or worse still, people may have to pay the price for a perceived short-term mistake. The safe and steady road, or acquiescence to the boss, are the only safe paths to follow.

The organisation as a garden, on the other hand, values diversity and appreciates that it is dealing with uncertainties and probabilities.

The organisation's Critical Leaders may not always make the 'best' decisions but they will make them the right way. Decisions are the result of an involvement with the Vital Connections including a dialogue with people, internally and externally. The involvement with Vital Connections encompassses the forces pulling the organisation to its preferred future—the culture, vision, values and work practices.

This dialogue is about 'what it means to work here' and focuses on adapting and growing the organisation to better meet the needs of all its stakeholders. It is a mere exchange of ideas or arriving at a new point through dialectics. The dialogue must be authentic and deep.

Agreement is not always required, but a demonstrated commitment to help people to be their best is essential. An abiding and genuine trust and respect for everybody in the organisation lies at the core of the decisions of Critical Leaders.

The ability to be involved in dialogue is a measure of the community-building that M. Scott Peck[6] argues must precede decision-making. While you should aspire to this, our experience also supports his contention that true communities are rare and that many Critical Leaders, especially those concerned with organisational transformation, must operate within the organisation as it is. What any Critical Leader can do is work with Vital Connections and achieve results with the people who truly understand the transformation and want to speed its process.

These Vital Connections are the people who will be involved in making decisions about the transformation and the work of Critical Leaders is to coach and support them in this process. Vital Connections may not always be able to arrive at consensus. The support of a shared preferred future does not mean that there will not be conflict and disagreement. At some stage, Critical Leaders recognise that the dialogue over a particular issue is weakening Vital Connections and will make a decision.

Such decisions require the commitment of the people willing and able to support the transformation to make them work. In an environment where there are no 'single best answers', and the patently wrong ones are those that will weaken or destroy the Vital Connections, the ability to celebrate and learn from mistakes is the other factor required to foster self-reliant decision-making.

The adaptation and growth that organisations need to survive will happen only if they learn from their own immediate experience and the experience of others. Learning is a major force within an organisation—it compels movement towards a preferred future. The capacity of the organisation to share experiences and learnings is a measure of its potential to prosper.

Deciding

Learning must be associated with the immediate experience. Critical Leaders must have the capacity for daily reflection as well as prompt action. Learning is a part of daily work, the daily experience. It must be related to contemporary relevant experiences. Decisions that are based upon things learned in earlier times may not be appropriate in the era of organisational quakes.

In *Competing for the Future*, Hamel and Prahalad write that an organisation must be prepared to 'unlearn' as well as learn:

To get to the future, a company must be willing to jettison, at least in part, its past . . . Creating the future doesn't require a company to abandon all of its past. Indeed a critical question for every firm is: What part of our past can be used as a 'pivot' to get to the future, and what part of our past represents excess baggage?[7]

Decisions must be made. The way forward then is to make decisions that help to create the future and to then reflect upon their success. If there are no penalties for making mistakes, Critical Leaders are able to focus on the future.[*]

James C. Collins and Jerry I. Porras researched 18 organisations that had outperformed the stock market by a factor of 15 since 1926 and one of their conclusions is that:

. . . if we had to bet our lives on the continued success and adaptability of any single company in our study over the next fifty to one hundred years, we would place that bet on 3M.[8]

They quote from a published history of 3M that considers the role of an early visionary manager who is attributed with establishing the foundation for the company's success. William McKnight, who was promoted to

---

[*] There is a lot to recommend about making mistakes. We refer the reader to 'Mistakes are a Good Investmnent' in Robert J. Kriegel and Louis Patler *If It Ain't Broke . . . Break It* and 'The Wallenda Factor' in Warren Bennis *An Invented Life*.

general manager while in his 20s in 1914, encouraged freedom and autonomy. He acknowledged of managers:

Mistakes will be made but . . . the mistakes he or she makes are not as serious in the long run as the mistakes management will make if it is dictatorial and undertakes to tell those under its authority exactly how they should do their job. Management that is destructively critical when mistakes are made kills initiative and it's essential that we have many people with initiative if we are to grow.[9]

Today in 3M people are encouraged to spend as much as 15 per cent of their time on any research project they wish, an approach that encourages self-reliance, decision-making and creativity. Creativity and innovation comes only from people who are capable of making decisions without fear. Of the organisation and its current CEO, *Fortune* magazine reported:

And 3M rarely lays off people. True, the company has fewer employees now (85 000) than ten years ago, when sales were only a third as big, but most of that decline came about through attrition. DeSimone (the CEO) figures that it's tough to fire a lot of people and then ask the innovators to stick their necks out and be innovative. And he questions the ability of managers who have had to cut their work forces deeply: 'Why did you get into a position that you had to lay off a bunch of people? How come you're so smart now that you've laid off a bunch of people?'[10]

Fear

Fear can be one of the greatest barriers to making decisions. The fear of rejection can prevent managers from acting. The fear of failure can paralyse

| Deciding |

whole systems.* It is encouraging to know that the leaders at Wal-Mart, a high performing organisation by any reckoning, meet:

> *... in an open forum every Saturday morning to discuss business and make decisions. The 300 managers applaud the week's top 25 stores and then get to work on the bottom 25. There's almost a perverse pride in acknowledging mistakes and correcting them.*[11]

Decision-making tools

Critical Leaders are not without help or tools to assist them make self-reliant decisions.

New ways of thinking

How we approach problems, issues or opportunities will affect the way we make decisions about them. Often we are limited by the perspective that we naturally bring because of the preferences in the way we think and make decisions, our past experiences and a thorough indoctrination in linear and sequential thinking.

The authors have used mind mapping and De Bono's 'Six Thinking Hats' to help groups to make decisions and plan actions. If the reader is interested in these techniques we recommend the books of Tony Buzan and Edward De Bono listed in the bibliography.

---

* One of Dr. W. Edwards Deming's Fourteen Points to greater performance is to 'Drive out Fear'. He maintained that management by results and other management practices put fear into the workplace and that the economic consequences of this are appalling. Another point was to put leadership into the workplace to help people be their best.

The All-Purpose Viewfinder

Weisbord's All-Purpose Viewfinder,[12] discussed in Chapter 7, is an excellent decision-making tool, providing a variety of perspectives through which to observe organisational issues. Marvin Weisbord created the Viewfinder to enable people to make decisions by looking at the whole system. Without looking at the whole system, the consequences of decisions may not be fully explored. The All-Purpose Viewfinder provides a link between the way the organisation is viewed and decision-making. If the focus is only internal, decisions will be made about people based upon a perception of them as a cost to the business. If the focus is also external, the organisation's people will be regarded as the source of profit and future strength.

In the words of Imparato and Harari, leaders must develop bi-focal vision in their organisations:

. . . to meet responsibilities to today's customers and investors, a leader must insist that today's products and processes be perfected. Simultaneously, to successfully meet the responsibilities to tomorrow's customers and investors, the company must work towards destroying the status quo in pursuit of the new . . . Every meeting agenda, memo, report and final decision should have a bi-focal dimension. That is, it should explicitly consider the impact on today's customers and tomorrow's. The weight in management meetings, even so-called routine meetings, should be on tomorrow.[13]

Making a difference

We have worked with organisations that are demanding that their people create more revenue but they are failing to provide the people with any sense of present or future security. They therefore fail to help the

| Deciding |

people to be the best they can be to help the organisation to adapt and grow.

Critical Leaders have an enormous capacity to make a difference at work through the decisions they make. They are responsible for the future of their organisations through both their own decisions and by helping other people to become self-reliant decision-makers.

Working with Vital Connections, they can ensure that decisions are purposeful and contribute to the capacity to build the preferred future.

Discovery

Decision-making

How does your organisation make decsions?

The machine   *The garden*

⟵─────────────────────⟶

Decisions are made slowly or avoided whenever possible | Decisions are made quickly

⟵─────────────────────⟶

There is no dialogue with the people about the whole business | There is an open and honest dialogue

⟵─────────────────────⟶

Decisions are mainly about the bottom line | Decisions are about the future including new customers and staff happiness

Roses and Rust

The machine	The garden
There is fear in the organisation	There is no fear and diversity of opinion is actively encouraged
There is little variation from the past—decisions are based on past practices	The organisation is prepared to 'unlearn' and take a risk
The people's 'consent' to decisions is not required; people will undermine decisions	The people's willing support of decisions, even those not agreed with, can be relied upon
People are blamed or punished for mistakes and errors of judgment	People are encouraged to learn from mistakes

9.
Helping

The art of leadership requires us to think about the leader-as-steward in terms of relationships: of assets and legacy, of momentum and effectiveness, of civility and values.

Max De Pree, CEO Herman Miller[1]

The wisdom of Max De Pree, a visionary leader whose organisation is renowned for both its profits and exemplary work practices, may seem a million miles from the world of business for many readers. However, it does not seem too fanciful to wish for such wisdom when you consider:

- The general manager of a national company said that when he wants to thank people he 'puts a clean nail in the four by two plank'. This manager had just received feedback on his leadership practices as perceived by ten peers and subordinates on Kouzes and Posner's Leadership Practices Inventory. Their ratings failed to place him on the grid in three out of five practices.
- The state manager of a sales team started a meeting with, 'Because of you ******* I didn't get a bonus.'
- The manager of a bank branch said, 'My people know when they are doing a good job because then I don't come out of my office.'

- A woman was told to cancel an important personal engagement to work back one evening, and was told by her manager, 'You can stay back because you don't have children to go home to.'

We know all of these managers. There are also nameless and countless others:

- who walk past the people who work for them and never acknowledge who they are
- who are never available to their people.

Many managers fail to engage themselves with their people—they fail to recognise and work with the Vital Connections and energies that exist between people and the organisation. At worst, they can cause a lot of harm as they damage people's commitment to the organisation and they destroy that sense of community that should be the foundation of any organisation. At best, they fail to enhance the performance of the organisation. Organisations grow through the people that work there. The organisation is its people and the Vital Connections they manage.

Critical Leaders define themselves by helping the people within the organisation to be their best. While the values behind helping people are fundamental and known to us all, enacting these through leadership still presents a challenge.

Redefining the meaning of work

The way people perceive work must change. That work should have a higher purpose than a pay cheque is unarguable but, by and large, the prevailing system of management has failed to provide that meaning.

The challenge facing Critical Leaders is to redefine the workplace. Critical Leadership is about serving the needs of all of the organisation's constituents. Their work must be redefined in terms of the 'preferred future' that they are working towards, and the Vital Connection with the customer.

The notion of a 'preferred future' was discussed in Chapter 4. What part does the 'preferred future' play in the process of helping people to be their best? The research of Kouzes and Posner in *The Leadership Challenge* found that exceptional leaders were able to inspire a shared vision with their people.

The Critical Leaders do precisely that with their people by building a picture of the future they want to create *together*. The preferred future is based upon their experiences and knowledge of the organisation and what they know can be achieved if they are engaged with their work.

The focus on the preferred future enables us to shift from focusing on what we are doing today to working for the future that we desire.

The practice of developing a preferred future with other people brings meaning to work and liberates people to do their best. It encompasses the consulting approach of Marvin Weisbord[2] who works with people to move:

Away from:
- solve the problem
- give it to an expert
- get a task force
- find the technique
- do it all now

Towards:
- create the future
- help each other learn
- involve everybody
- find a valued purpose
- do what's do-able—in season.

Critical Leaders can facilitate the creation of a preferred future by establishing with their people the 'valued purpose' that comes from working with Vital Connections.

The organisation's unit of value today is the Vital Connection with the customer. Organisations are all in the business of providing service, and customer attraction and loyalty are the key to an organisation's survival and growth.

It seems that this is theoretically well accepted everywhere but at the level of the actual service provider.

Many organisations continue to treat both the internal and the external customer poorly. It is little wonder in their research on organisations that deliver extraordinary results, Kotter and Heskett were able to conclude:

In most firms, managers do not care deeply about customers and stockholders and employees. They may value one of their constituency groups, or perhaps even two, but not all three. More likely, they have been taught to care more about their kind of work (accounting, engineering, etc.), their department, specific products, or only themselves.[3]

Managing all these constituency groups is the key to extraordinary performance.

The Australian experience is no better than the American. T. J. Larkin reports the findings of research sponsored by the National Training Council (NTC) in 1986:

[Research] . . . concentrated on over-the-counter service staff such as: postal clerks, driver examiners, bank tellers, insurance claims officers and waiters/ waitresses. Through questionnaires and discussion groups the NTC revealed that a staggering 50 per cent of these employees described themselves as 'indifferent' in their dealing with customers. When it comes to customers half of our counter staffs in banks, restaurants, insurance companies, travel agencies, hotels and the like just couldn't care less . . .

Australian employees believe that their job is to do tasks, not serve customers.[4]

There has been progress in some sectors since the NTC research, perhaps notably in some public sector bodies where the NTC recorded that 80 per cent of employees expressed 'indifference' or were 'even more negative' to the customer.

However, at the beginning of 1995, the TARP Corporation released research commissioned by the Society of Consumer Affairs Professionals that identified that most Australians 'had to complain about four times before getting results . . .'[5]

There seems to be little evidence of executives demonstrating a commitment to customers, apart from generating important-sounding words on countless and forgettable statements of vision/mission/purpose. It is little wonder that counter service staff have not embraced the idea of customer service.

(We once asked a workshop of the 12 executives of an organisation of 18 000 people what the three key one sentence statements were in their mission statement—no one responded.)

These results are sad and illuminating. The continuing waves of customer service training and corporate messages about being 'customer driven' just don't work. The organisation's *ethos* has to be customer driven, as it is in companies such as Nordstrom and Ritz-Carlton.

The Critical Leader has to help people redefine their work *before* interventions such as training are planned. The research reported by T.J. Larkin demonstrates that people know how to serve customers, they just don't want to.

In an article on customer service, Sandra Vandermerwe, a professor at the International Institute for management development in Lausanne, Switzerland, presents the argument that:

. . . just as many primitive, tribal languages describe objects in terms of what they do instead of what they are, companies should think of products in terms of what they accomplish.[6]

The work that people do must be described in terms of its intent—the impact it will have on the customer. The ongoing tasks in the job must be described in terms of the relationship with the customer. Whether that customer is internal or external is irrelevant.

The 'moment of truth' is a sound foundation for guiding behaviour. People must do whatever has to be done to maximise the value added to the customer. Whether it is described as a 'passion for customers' or whether it is as direct as Jack Welch stating that 'companies can't give job security, only customers can',[7] work must only be described in customer benefit terms.

The Vital Connection with customers must become the deep and abiding purpose for work. By aligning this purpose to the preferred future, the Critical Leader begins to harness the syzygy to bring out the best in people.

We have found that when the picture of the preferred future is established and work has started with the primary Vital Connection of people who are willing to support the transformation, there is no difficulty at all finding people who wish to enlist to the cause.

Core competencies in the organisation also need to be defined in customer relationship terms.

Core competencies

Every organisation must be able to express what makes it unique in terms that are meaningful to customers. It should be able to say why the organisation is needed. To do this organisations need to be able to develop the competencies that will enable it to distinguish itself from its environment. The ability to be adaptive and flexible so that it is able to respond rapidly to changes in this environment is an example of such a core competency.

A 'core competence' has been defined by Hamel and Prahalad as:

... a bundle of skills and technologies rather than a single discrete skill or technology ... A core competence must make a disproportionate contribution to customer-perceived value. Core competencies are the skills that enable a firm to deliver a fundamental customer benefit.[8]

Customers must be able to distinguish and appreciate the value that a particular organisation contributes to their lives. All the people within an organisation must be able to identify with the core competencies that enable the organisation to add value uniquely to its customers.

Successful organisations will develop core competencies, and be able to establish that these are what they have to offer the marketplace. The nature of core competencies can range from specific technologies to the organisation's approach to its customers.

In the early 1980s, Cheryl Womack started a company that sells insurance to independent truck drivers.[9] It has grown from a one-person operation to a company with a staff of 70 people—'all but nine are women'—and revenues of more than $US25 million. The core competencies of her organisation include:

- 'a string of innovative insurance products' including at least one that no one else had applied to the trucking industry before
- people with 'passion, flexibility and excitement'.

When the core competencies are known, they provide the basis for the recruitment and development of staff. In Cheryl Womack's company '95 per cent of innovations come from the employees'. This is the outcome of hiring those people who are able to deliver on the organisation's core competencies.

Critical Leaders are often not the executives of organisations. They frequently have to work with what is rather than what should be. They are still able to develop core competencies with their work units, irrespective of the total organisational picture.

They do this by developing a shared picture of how the work unit is able to deliver 'a fundamental customer benefit' by considering how it can apply the five dimensions of service, as revealed in Table 9.1 (in order of importance to customers).[10] Exceeding the expectations of customers on these dimensions and a commitment to continuously improving them are fundamental to long-term organisational success.

When customers judge the 'moment of truth' it is the organisation's performance on these dimensions that will determine the outcome of that judgment.

Table 9.1 The five dimensions of service

1.	*Reliability:*	the ability to perform the promised service dependably and accurately
2.	*Responsiveness:*	the willingness to help customers and provide prompt service
3.	*Assurance:*	the knowledge and courtesy of employees and their ability to convey trust and competence
4.	*Empathy:*	the caring, individualised attention provided to the customer
5.	*Tangibles:*	the appearance of physical facilities, equipment, personnel and communication material

Source: A. Parasuraman, Valarie Zeithaml and Leonard L. Berry (1986) 'Servqual: A Multiple-Item Scale for Measuring Customer Perceptions of Service Quality', Working Paper of the Marketing Science Institute Research Program, Cambridge, Mass.

The Critical Leader has to facilitate the work unit's ability to deliver service on these dimensions, removing the barriers to people doing the work that has to be done.

Redefining the meaning of work and developing core competencies provide a foundation for the Critical Leader to focus on developing performance.

Role perception

The research of Kotter and Heskett[11] identified that organisations that looked after their people outperformed, by a huge margin, those that did not. Looking after people is helping them to be their best.

Helping

The work of Nicholas Imparato and Oren Harari has been of great importance in determining how we can help people to improve workplace performance. In *Jumping the Curve*[12] they question the 'so-called truths about the critical arena of individual performance'. Performance has traditionally been defined as an outcome of two variables, ability and motivation.[13] This could be expressed as a formula, $P = A \times M$. Imparato and Harari have added one more variable to the formula—Accuracy of Role Perception (*ARP*).

> The formula for performance becomes:
>
> $P = A \times M \times ARP$

The need for this modification became clear to them when they were looking at managers who were successful agents of change.

While other managers had the ability and competence their jobs demanded, outstanding managers were those who perceived their role to encompass attributes that included, among others, embracing change, attending to external realities, promoting a coaching style and expanding job responsibilities.

The ability and motivation of managers may be related to a perception of the organisation only as they have known it, and not what it must become in response to future demands:

. . . the tumultuous changes around us demand new behaviours and actions, a new way of defining our role as manager. Without the appropriate role perception, performance is depressed, ability and motivation notwithstanding, because managers do not take on the responsibility to act in ways that are in harmony with the demands of the emerging epoch. Without accuracy of role perception, all the advice and how-to's in the world have little impact. An inaccurate role perception explains why so many managers who attend seminars and listen to management tapes can't translate their knowledge into higher performance back on the job.[14]

The factors that determine the role perception of managers will vary from organisation to organisation. But they should always include helping the organisation to grow and adapt, and helping people to be the best they can be.

In General Electric, the top 200 or so managers are rated on their performance according to the organisation's shared values, which include 'candor, speed, and self-confidence'.[15] As these are the shared values that guide the organisation, the managers have a very clear perception of what is expected of them.

What holds true for managers is valid for people at all levels and in all roles in the organisation. Helping to clarify the perception that people have of their role becomes part of the work of Critical Leaders, part of 'defining the reality' (as Max De Pree calls it), especially in times of transformation and organisational quakes.

People will naturally hold on to the perception of the job that they were hired to do. Their perception may not change as the job changes unless the Critical Leader or manager assists with this change in perception. This will be particularly true of organisations that place credence in job descriptions and instruction manuals.

The research reported by Larkin, and that undertaken more recently by TARP, indicates that many organisations have neither developed service as a core competency nor do the staff perceive it as a part of their role. Customers are left to deal with the fact that the people and management in most organisations define their work by the processes in which they participate rather than by care for their customers.

The impact of the new formula in explaining performance cannot be underestimated. At a workshop to develop sales plans for a work unit in a major Australian bank, the issue of the team's performance was raised. We considered the formula, which can be used to rank both team and individual performance. (This exercise is worth conducting with teams.)

Discussing the role

What does your role mean in these turbulent times? In the workshop we discussed what it meant to sell in the bank. The group agreed on answers, such as spotting and qualifying opportunities, identifying unarticulated needs and questioning and listening to customers.

At this stage of the workshop we encountered a stumbling block—what did the executive of the bank really expect these people to do?

Giving a rating

Next a rating out of ten for each of the variables—Ability, Motivation and Accuracy of Role Perception—should be given. Performance is then expressed as a possible maximum score of 1000 (maximum $P = 10 \times 10 \times 10$).

Scoring the outcome

The group was doing well until this point. Their equation was:

$$P = 9 \times 8 \times 5$$

That is: $P = 360/1000$

The basis for the group's scoring was as follows:

- Ability was 9, as the average time in the job was over 20 years.
- Motivation was 8, a little lower than they would have liked, but there had been continuous restructures and some retrenchments.
- Accuracy of Role Perception was 5, as there had been frequent changes in leadership—what did this new boss want? Will this talk about selling be a flash in the pan?

Their performance was little more than a third of what it could have been. One person retorted, 'But we're better than that.' As Imparato and Harari note:

The multiplication signs [in the formula $P = A \times M \times ARP$] indicate that the effects of the ability, motivation, and role perception are noncompensating:

a high score in one dimension can't compensate for a low score in another. In the extreme, if both ability and motivation were a 10 and accuracy of role perception were a 0, performance would be wiped out.[16]

With each of the variables impacting on each of the others, the workshop group could be rated no better than their score of 360. A higher score was not possible when the work, their role, had not been defined *with them*. And without such definition they were unable to translate into action the behaviours that would lead to high performance.

The group could not be the 'best they could be' until their role perception was addressed. The workshop decided that training and other interventions would not have been appropriate at that time.

For these reasons, the Critical Leader must establish the syzygy between the preferred future, the role perception and the core competencies—these are forces that can transform the organisation and pull it into the future.

Motivation

The power of Imparato and Harari's performance formula is that it establishes that all the variables are related. Motivation is linked to both role perception and ability. An individual's or a team's motivation depends upon whether they have a shared and accurate perception of their role and of their ability to accomplish the organisation's goals.

The issue of motivation causes a great deal of concern with managers, particularly as they feel that the issue has been high-jacked by amateur behaviourists. When performance of organisations has suffered in times of organisational quakes managers have looked for reasons or excuses for the failure of people to switch to new behaviours and practices.

When one major bank failed to get its managers out of their branches and into the offices and workplaces of customers, it offered a

$25 'reward' for each customer visit. The result? A lot of visits because that was what was being rewarded. The reward produced movement, not motivation. This is an example of management's search for a technique to motivate people rather than focusing on creating the environment where people choose to motivate themselves, grow and learn and be their best.

All the research into pay for performance and incentive schemes[17] has identified that, although 75 to 90 per cent of US businesses tie compensation to performance with raises, bonuses, cash and the like, these schemes ultimately lead to inferior work and a focus on short-term results. Such short-term focus is the antithesis of building a preferred future and strong Vital Connections with customers. It is, as we've heard Ken Blanchard say, 'like playing tennis by watching the score board instead of the ball'.*

The faith in rewards as a way of motivating people stems from the influence of Skinnerian behaviourism. B. F. Skinner believed that human behaviour was a product of external influences and that it was possible to program learning and behaviour in order to produce an ideal planned society. (We refer the reader to Alfie Kohn's account of Skinner and behaviourism.) Ultimately this reduces the art of management to the simplistic offering of carrots and sticks.

This return to a Theory X view of people at work is ultimately dehumanising and degrading.

Theory X and Theory Y

In 1960 Douglas McGregor published *The Human Side of Enterprise*. He hoped to promote a greater degree of co-operation between management and labour in order to bring about workplace change. After 30 years, it is still abundantly clear that most organisations fail to engage the hearts and minds of their people or enlist their trust and support.

---

* An address to the American Society of Training and Development 48th National Conference, New Orleans, 1992.

Theory X and Theory Y, as developed by McGregor, represent fundamental differences in approach to the people at work. Theory X will destroy the Vital Connection with and between the people; Theory Y will engage people as Vital Connections. The essence of each approach is captured in Table 9.2.

Theory Y also unlocks the key to motivation:

- changing the way people are treated will do more for productivity than changing the way they are paid
- it is not possible to motivate other people to improve their long-term performance
- Critical Leaders can create the conditions whereby people may choose to motivate themselves.

When people choose to motivate themselves we speak of 'intrinsic' motivation. These people find their work to be inherently rewarding. Alfie Kohn found that:

Intrinsically motivated people . . . pursue optimal challenges, display greater innovativeness, and tend to perform better under challenging circumstances.[18]

Although Critical Leaders recognise that no one can motivate others, they are able to establish the context that helps people by:

. . . setting up certain conditions that will maximise the probability of their developing an interest in what they are doing and remove the conditions that function as constraints.[19]

These 'certain conditions' are no more magical than being involved with the Vital Connections and caring for people's welfare, establishing a sense of meaning and excitement about a preferred future. As Hamel and Prahalad note:

The more excited a worker is, the less are remuneration and hygiene factors the sole barriers of contentment. In high-drama, high-purpose organisations

Table 9.2 McGregor's Theory X and Theory Y

Theory X assumptions:
- People are lazy, dislike work and will try to avoid it if possible.
- People lack ambition, prefer to be led and dislike responsibility.
- Punishment must be used to get people to achieve organisational goals.
- People will resist change.
- People lack creativity and want security above all.

This leads to the following management behaviours:
- Management is responsible for organising, planning and important decision-making.
- Management directs people.
- If management doesn't act, then employees won't do much; therefore it is management's responsibility to motivate employees.
- Management can't trust employees with important decisions.

Theory Y assumptions:
- People are ambitious and work is natural.
- People seek responsibility and self-control in achieving goals.
- People recognise and accept organisation goals.
- People are dynamic and flexible.
- People are intelligent and possess creative potential. Most businesses don't use this potential.

This leads to the following management behaviours:
- Management can delegate important decisions to lower levels.
- With the right kinds of leadership, employees won't be passive or resistant.
- Employees have the ability to be high performers, to develop, to assume responsibility and are self-motivated. Therefore, management only has to set up the right working conditions to bring all these abilities together.
- Management can trust employees.

like Data General in the early years . . . excitement often runs roughshod over satisfaction (with pay and conditions).[20]

While organisations must 'pay for value', they do not need to destroy the opportunity to develop an environment that promotes intrinsic motivation by developing a 'carrots and sticks' approach to remuneration.*

A wonderful example of establishing these 'certain conditions' comes from the American management of Honda Motor Co. Ltd (US) who broadcast and promote the following five value statements as their management policy:

- Proceed always with ambition and youthfulness.
- Respect sound theory, develop fresh ideas, and make the most effective use of time.
- Enjoy your work, and always brighten the working atmosphere.
- Strive constantly for a harmonious flow of work.
- Be ever mindful of the value of research and endeavour.[21]

The managers at Honda promise to their people that at least there should not be barriers to people being their best and that the working atmosphere should be a happy one.

When the *One Minute Manager* was written in 1983 it contained the 'simple truth' of the manager who 'laughed, worked, and enjoyed'. That simple truth has been lost in organisations. It is there for Critical Leaders to rediscover and to use to bring harmony and fun to the process of transformation.

---

* It is worth noting that every survey that has been undertaken in Australia regarding what people see as important at workplaces places good pay after factors such as 'job allows achievement', 'is interesting', 'provides security', 'provides opportunity for initiative' and 'pleasant colleagues'. Examples of these surveys can be found in Frederick G. Hilmer (1989) *New Games, New Rules—Work in Competitive Enterprises*, Sydney: Angus & Robertson, p. 77. Similar results for the US are reported in Kouzes and Posner, *The Leadership Challenge*, p. 77.

Ability

Of the variables in the performance formula we have left ability until last, and with good reason. The typical response of managers in machine organisations is to 'fix' problems with a training intervention. Until appropriate and accurate role perceptions and the conditions to promote motivation are established, focusing on the ability of people is a fruitless exercise.

Many years ago, as an overall organisational service quality initiative, we were asked to improve the telephone answering skills of the office staff in an organisation that employed 350 people over a dispersed site. We noticed two things that meant we would not offer a telephone courtesy training program. The first was that no one in the organisation would answer any phone that wasn't their own. The receptionist would transfer calls and if the person was not at their desk the phone would go unanswered until it transferred back to her.

The second problem was that when some calls were transferred they would go into a loop which meant that they could go to three extensions before they transferred back to the switchboard. When this occurred, the switchboard operator was unable to distinguish it from an in-coming call—the customer was greeted as though for the first time.

It is little wonder that there were a lot of customer complaints about the telephone service. Making it everyone's role to pick up unattended phones and take messages reduced the calls to the receptionist by over 30 per cent. The number of complaints fell markedly and virtually disappeared when the organisation replaced its communication technology.

We do not maintain that skill development is inconsequential. It is indeed vital—but it has its appropriate place in the scheme of things.

Another typical approach in the machine organisation is for *managers* to decide upon the abilities they wish to see developed. The approach of the Critical Leader is to provide *people* with the opportunity to decide how they can indeed learn to become the 'best'. This approach goes beyond the traditional needs analysis that aims to identify the gap between the current skills and the desired skills of the workforce or an individual. Working with Vital Connections means that people decide what they need to know to do their jobs and they decide when and how they can best learn.

When Critical Leaders work with their people to develop a picture of a preferred future, they enable the people to identify the skills and attributes they will require to help themselves to grow in the job and to help the organisation to grow and adapt.

Performance—the machine and the garden

The formula for performance ($P = A \times M \times ARP$) can be applied in both the machine organisation and the adaptive organisation—the organisation as a garden. The machine organisation fails, however, to explore the complexity of performance. Performance in such organisations is generally regarded as the outcome of a 'download' to the people: 'Here's training (A), some rewards or punishments (M), and your job description (ARP)—go and do likewise.' The manager then ceases to take responsibility for developing performance; either the people get it right as a result of the manager's intervention, or they are the 'wrong people'.

In the garden organisation, performance issues are much more complex and more realistic. Performance is the result of the Critical Leader and the people working together to optimise performance by an involvement in numerous variables. For the role of manager, for example, Imparato and Harari offered at least 13 factors that impacted upon accuracy of role perception of managers in periods of transformation. These are quite apart from the variables that are involved in determining ability and motivation.

Figure 9.1 contrasts the simplistic machine understanding of performance with the complexity of the garden.

Figure 9.1 Comparing performance

$P = A \times M \times ARP$

In the machine:

$P =$	A	$\times$	M	$\times$	ARP
	Where A is:		Where M is:		Where ARP is:
	• training		• carrots and sticks		• job descriptions

In the garden:

$P =$	A	$\times$	M	$\times$	ARP
	Where A is:		Where M is:		Where ARP is:
	• skills		• desires		• embracing change
	• intelligence		• goals		• developing expertise
	• aptitude		• incentives		• keeping life balance
	• talents		• preferences		• providing feedback
			• sense of community		• improving the workplace
			• ownership of work		• Critical Leadership
					• modelling best practices
					• supporting the team

For specific workplaces in a garden organisation the elements that constitute each variable of the equation will change. The table does however include those that we believe are applicable to all people. It is particularly important in regard to accuracy of role perception that people embrace change in their work, have opportunities to develop expertise, keep a sense of proportion with work and other parts of their lives, demonstrate Critical Leadership and have a customer driven approach to their work.

Vital Connections and the community of work

The Critical Leader can help people become their best by strengthening the Vital Connections to build a sense of community within the organisation. The strengthening of those Vital Connections engages the people to contribute to achieving the preferred future.

In a group we once worked with, a manager said, in exasperation, 'Give me the room to do the job you asked me to do.' If the customer is defined as a Vital Connection, people must be allowed to do what has to be done to grow and strengthen that connection.

Instead we often find managers erecting bureaucracies and applying rules and systems that make it difficult, if not impossible, to do the work that has to be done.

Organisational hierarchies, talking only to direct reports, making decisions at the top and expecting other people, the subordinates, to implement them, sap energy out of the forces that bind the organisation together.

Organisations such as 3M actively promote the working relationships that we identify as Vital Connections. In so doing, they have promoted empowerment and a sense of community. The three following points are among the tenets for 'managing and motivating people' of Livio DeSimone, 3M's CEO, who:

- encourages people to follow their interest
- creates a culture of co-operation
- stages a lot of celebrations.[22]

As we noted earlier, people in 3M are free to devote 15 per cent of their time to any research project they wish. 'Some techies spend not just 15 per cent but 50 per cent of their time pursuing dream ideas; managers are encouraged to let them do so.'[23]

This practice has enabled 3M to be at the forefront of product and technology development for everything from post-it notes (developed in the free time of its co-inventor, Art Fry, who 'wanted little adhesive papers to mark the hymns he was going to sing at Sunday church services; he thought of co-inventor Spence Silver, who had developed a light adhesive) to sophisticated communications technology.

Everybody at 3M is encouraged to call up any other employee and tap into that person's expertise . . . And part of that person's job is to freely share such knowledge—on the phone, by E-mail, in person, or any other way.

The company recognises success not so much by giving shares or bonuses but by holding events where peers cheer peers. Honorees get a certificate and a backpat from Desi, and waves of applause.[24]

While we are not suggesting that Australian companies hold the equivalent of 3M's Oscar night, the case for developing Vital Connections and celebrating success is the cornerstone of building a community in the organisation.

Critical Leaders recognise that the people who best know how to do the work are also the best people to undertake its transformation to an adaptive culture. It is crucial to facilitate the establishment of connections between all the people within an organisation.

This means liberating the leader within everyone. The Critical Leader must be obsessed with gaining the full participation of people. Everyone has ideas for how they would do the job better. For people to be effective they should be able to act on these ideas rather than seeking permission to do something.

This also removes the political games and power plays that sap energy out of the business. Giving everyone power means that no one seeks it from others. Instead of trying to find ways to get power over other people, everyone looks for ways of helping each other for a known and common purpose.

Another way that Critical Leaders can remove the barriers to people being their best is to enable free access to information. Everyone must have free access to whatever information they decide they need to know. This is the opposite of the pervasive military notion that people should get information on a 'need to know' basis.

Most supervisors think that part of their role is to shield their subordinates from bad news coming down from above. When we shield our people we are acting as their parents and treating them like children. If we are trying to create the mindset that everyone is responsible for the success of this business then our people need complete information.[25]

People must have access to information even about the financial side of the business if they are to help it to grow and adapt. There is no other way for the organisation to achieve success.

In the organisation as a garden or living entity, people must focus on building the community, the whole organisation. Managers in machine organisations will focus on developing internal competition for rewards and benefits; Critical Leaders in garden organisations will focus on building the power of all the people to help the organisation grow. Rather than competing for pieces of the cake in the machine organisation, the people will be encouraged to make the cake bigger and share, as a community, in the organisation's success.

On reflection

Although there are no off-the-shelf prescriptions for helping people to be the best they can be, recognising the need and the path to follow is the only possible start.

The people are not the 'human resource' of the organisation—because they participate in Vital Connections they *are* the organisation. Their ability to forge viable Vital Connections with each other and customers will reward the organisation. And perhaps then the organisation will begin to share the wonder and joy of its success.

Discovery

Helping

The machine	The garden
'Thank God it's Friday!'	'Thank God it's Monday!'
'Get a task force'	'Involve everybody'
People are 'indifferent' to customers	People go out of their way to exceed customer expectations
Managers rely on job descriptions	People do what has to be done
Carrots and sticks are used to 'motivate' people	The work is intrinsically motivating
People feel as though they are not paid fair value for the work they do	People feel as though they are paid fairly
People do not share an accurate perception of their role	People share an accurate perception of their role

Roses and Rust

The machine	*The garden*
Performance is low	Performance is high
People resist change	People are dynamic and flexible
There is little co-operation or help	Co-operation and help occur everywhere and between organisational levels

10.
Energy

Once upon a time, a kindergarten in Connecticut developed a mission statement: 'Be the best you can be.' After a time, they decided that this was not quite right. Being the best was not worth it, if it meant being cruel or unfair to others. So they amended their mission statement by adding: '. . . and be nice'.

Bob Newton, an old friend

The model of Critical Leadership tells us that the Critical Leader must focus on helping the people of the organisation to be the best they can be. The *quid pro quo* of this is that the people of the organisation help the organisation to adapt and grow. We do not believe that this process works without an ethical approach to developing the business and working with the people. This approach is the way to harnessing the energy of the people.

An ethical approach to transforming an organisation must focus on the three constituents:

- the people who work in the organisation
- the people who are the customers of the organisation
- the people who have invested in the organisation.

This ethical approach must clearly state: 'Yes, we make a profit, but not at any cost!'

This chapter explores the transforming organisation, and the costs associated with success 'at any price'. It takes the view of the Connecticut kindergarten: 'Be the best you can be . . . and be nice'. 'Being nice' is about:

- being deeply committed to being the best
- developing genuine respect, trust and kindness at work
- creating work that has worth
- strengthening Vital Connections by bringing energy to them.

It is not about being wimpy or avoiding being firm. On the contrary, it embraces Max De Pree's two key responsibilities of leadership:

The first responsibility of leadership is to define reality. The last is to say thank you.[1]

It has been said that organisations exist in order to exist. The business must be looked after if it is to stay in business. Caretakers of the organisation who do not watch the cash flow of the business are not doing any favours for its constituents. But the manager who watches only the cash flow and does not nourish the needs, hopes and dreams of the people has also failed to recognise the reality that the people and the Vital Connections they participate in *are* the organisation.

The people will accept almost any reality about the organisation if they are treated with dignity, respect and kindness.

A little respect goes a long way

We worked with a sales team in a major organisation over a period of 15 months. You are already familiar with this team's manager, who during that time once greeted them with, 'Because of you *******, I didn't get a bonus.' This manager was replaced by someone unknown to the team.

Energy

Within the first month of his appointment he shared with the team the sales goal that he had been given by the company's executive. The task was enormous—the goal was well beyond the original budget expectations for the next two years.

Yet the new manager succeeded in gaining the support of the team. He 'defined reality'—this has to be done, we have to change and do business differently, and these are the boundaries you can operate in. Then he invited the people to join the effort, determining how *they* thought it could best be done and how they would share their success. This process occurred over a workshop that ran for a day and a half. Two days after it was completed one of the managers rang a colleague at 4.30 in the morning because he had so many good ideas about what to do that he could not wait to discuss them.

The 'hard' values of business growth were communicated bluntly and honestly; so too were the 'soft' values of respect and caring for the people in the organisation and their customers. The message about the business succeeded *because* there was a corresponding message about the people. Both messages were delivered with passion and excitement.

There is an impediment to optimising performance in most machine organisations, including the organisation above. The alarming truth is that most people do not feel valued at work. A survey of 500 000 workers in the US Postal Service reported that only a quarter felt that they were treated with respect and dignity. Many surveys have indicated that only 25–50 per cent of the people at work feel as though they have been treated with respect and dignity.

Even more alarming is that managers are asking people to do more to help the organisation when the people are clearly not feeling valued or respected. In the absence of dignity and respect there can be no strong Vital Connections between the people and the customers, between the people and the organisation's need to grow and adapt, and between the present and the preferred future of the organisation.

'Soft' values are clearly more important than their epithet suggests. They are the values that bring energy into the workplace and strength to the Vital Connections. They cause the syzygy between the organisation's governance, its people and the preferred future. They determine the structure, because the organisation will be formed along the lines and energies that maximise syzygy with the environment. They also determine the practices that enable the organisation to flourish as a garden rather than function as a machine. And in turn, they determine the purpose and meaning of the work.

In his work *What Life Could Mean To You*, Alfred Adler tells us that 'Human beings live in the realm of meanings.'[2] Adler goes further, and instructs us that we are all dealing with three constraints which leave each and every one of us with three problems to solve:

... first, how to find an occupation that will enable us to survive under the limitations set by the nature of our home planet; secondly, how to find a position among our fellow human beings, so that we can co-operate and share the benefits of co-operation; and thirdly, how to accommodate ourselves to the fact that there are two sexes and that the continuance of mankind depends upon the relations between them[3]

Coming to work should be part of finding the solutions to the problems which Adler suggests we must solve—not part of the problem. Unhappily, when managers regard their people as a human resource and cost centre, they fail to consider the value that a person's vocation and ability to support loved ones has for them. Families and loved ones suffer the consequences of re-engineering and restructures that would not have been required if the organisation had been responsive to its environment, and its people engaged in helping it to adapt and grow. Adler's second 'problem', the need to find a place to share the benefits of co-operation, is also denied by managers as they break Vital Connections in their continuing focus on the restructuring of machine organisations. While Adler's focus in the third problem was on the continuance of humanity rather than organisational development, it is fair to say that the relationship between men and women has not been fairly resolved in terms of participation, influence and power at work.

Energy

Integrity at work

Organisations must speak about their values—what it means to work here—about how they wish to be known to their people, their customers and their other stakeholders. Some companies such as The Body Shop proudly define and successfully promote their core values. (These values appear at the end of the chapter.) However, the people of most organisations have received too many conflicting messages on values, especially if they have been told that they are the organisation's most important resource.* We could guess at the number of organisations that have said 'We are our people', only to withdraw such a statement symbolically through their re-engineering efforts and retrenchments.

'Integrity' is proclaimed as a core value of most companies. However, in some organisations it could be suggested that this core value might be operating by the J. R. Ewing definition: 'Once you give up integrity, the rest is a piece of cake.'

We will not name the organisation because its involvement in past practices of dubious integrity are not a fair reflection of what it is today, but it is still exciting to recall the national manager who confronted those practices with his team, and said, 'From this point onwards, I am inviting you to judge me by the integrity of my dealings with employees and customers—and I expect the same of you.' The atmosphere in the room was electric as the managers heard, for the first time, a message that was not about the financials but about an organisation that was being driven by values and a high purpose. The room and its people were filled with an energy that had never been there before.

Some months later in the same organisation, a manager told the national manager that he would have once sacrificed his family and personal life in favour of his career. This occurred when the managers met to

---

*We recommend that you duck if you hear this remark from anyone above your supervising manager—except if your supervising manager is the CEO, then our advice stands without qualification.

discuss only one item—their values, as people and as a team. The manager received the full support of his boss and the rest of the team. The organisation had redefined what it meant to work there.

Critical Leaders are required to help focus their organisations on the need to bridge the gap between what *is* and what *should be* at work. Organisations have to practise integrity *before* they talk about it to their people. We have been given far too many reasons to be cynical about the talk. Many people have written of the 'excesses' of the 1980s. 'Excess' is scarcely an adequate description. It was more appropriately described by one writer who noted:

> *... the sheer scale and frequency of dubious transactions is breathtaking ... it is the arrogance and indifference that really sticks in my craw.*[4]

Responsibility and remuneration

While the dubious practices may have declined, the arrogance and indifference has yet to depart. The people within most organisations are treated little better than cogs in a machine. Instead of creating the environment for people to be their best and to develop their interest and commitment to the work, to bring energy to their work, managers try to change their behaviour by manipulating the pay systems and offering rewards and inducements.

The way people are paid should be in accord with the values of the organisation. The pay system of an organisation that recognises Vital Connections will be very different from that of the machine organisation which offers incentives and rewards in exchange for a change in behaviour. As noted in Chapter 6, the focus must be on an intrinsically rewarding workplace where all the people share in the success of the whole organisation, not just the few who maintain a position in the hierarchy.

Arrogance and indifference to the people in organisations is surely continuing when it is noted that, while the 'workers' are being retrenched or are given minimal increases in pay, the people at the top are voting themselves unprecedented pay increases and access to privileges. This is a reflection of the machine organisation.

The executives are paying themselves for the additional weight and pressure they face in carrying the organisation on their shoulders. There is no argument with this. However it is clear that in most organisations that the strategy of the people at the top is to pay themselves as much as possible.

The organisation as a garden recognises that the weight and responsibility for the success of the organisation rests with everyone. While the people at the top continue to be paid more, these organisations acknowledge, through their pay systems, the weight and responsibility that the people, at all levels, share for the organisation's success.

The present pay systems in most organisations do not reflect this shared responsibility. Peter Block describes the distribution curves that are used to determine how much people are paid:

Without getting into graphs, it works out that the people rated in the bottom ten per cent are given minimal or zero increase, the people rated in the top ten per cent are given maximum increase, usually about four per cent higher than inflation, and everyone else is placed in the middle. Everyone has to be force-fitted into this bell-shaped curve. In other words, only ten per cent can be called top performers, and ten per cent must be called poor performers. If you are a manager and think 20 per cent of your people are top performers, you have an Olympic-sized battle on your hands. This restraint, though, does not apply for people at the top three levels. They have a different system, reinforcing the belief that we are dealing with two different classes of people.[5]

Making people fit a distribution curve is not treating them with dignity and respect. It fails to recognise the commitment that people make to their organisations, a commitment that cannot be measured by money alone. It also fails to recognise the need of people to 'achieve and connect' and it debases their lives in a 'realm of meaning'. It does not encourage people to be their best. On the contrary, it is likely to demotivate people, as it measures their worth on a meaningless scale.*

Only machine organisations would feel the need to put people and their pay onto a distribution curve. It becomes another picture for the managers to demonstrate that their machine is running smoothly and in accord with the performance as it is depicted on charts for 'vehicles of a similar class'. When managers do this, they are unwittingly but surely subverting the organisation's ability to grow and make money. Paying people on the basis of a predetermined distribution scale focuses people on competing for the share of the cake they will get. Critical Leaders shift the focus on growing the total cake—the organisation must adapt and grow—and everyone shares in the result.

Dignity under pressure

If ethics provide the meaning for us, we are then able to factor all aspects of the work we do in human terms. This becomes even more important when organisations are facing difficult times and experiencing setbacks in their efforts. Stress and failure creates pressure on the organisation. It is in these times that an organisation's approach to survival tells whether or not it believes that 'being nice'—making decisions fairly and ethically—is appended to the necessity of being the best.

When things get tough within your organisation, how do people act? When the pressure is really on, what happens? We don't know the right answer to this question, but should the organisation survive no matter how much prolonged pain the people experience? Somehow it is hard to imagine an organisation telling its people, 'That's it! It prolongs the misery too much—we are going to abandon ship.'

The pain often signals an opportunity for the organisation to transform itself. In Victoria, a fruit processing plant was facing the choice of closure or an ongoing bitter argument between the unions and the

---

* Distribution curves were not meant to measure everything. In the context of determining levels of pay a distribution curve is an arbitrary scale.

owners about how to continue to operate the plant while it was making enormous losses. The workers took the debate into their own hands and, contrary to union advice, voted themselves reductions in pay and working conditions. Within a short time, they turned the plant around and recouped all the benefits they had lost.

Why do we deny basic humanness at work? Is the image of organisational CEOs sitting in the war room, plotting the next hill to conquer an appropriate image? Is it okay to say, 'Well, that hill only cost us 30 lives?' Is it morally acceptable to know stress levels within all organisations have gone through the roof? Still we restructure. And still we retrench. People lose their livelihood for mistakes they did not make. And still we talk about 'just getting on with it'. Still we don't get it right.

Are actions in the name of the shareholder, even those which harm the people who work for the organisation, okay? Are actions that increase the wealth of the few, whether they are shareholders or executives, and deny a fair pay system for the many acceptable?

Many thinkers and writers are drawing the attention of organisations to the need to develop leaders who have strong personal values.[6] 'A leader,' write Kouzes and Posner:

... needs a philosophy, a set of high standards by which the organisation is measured, a set of values about how employees, colleagues, and customers ought to be treated, a set of principles that make the organisation unique and distinctive ... Leaders stand up for their beliefs. They practice what they preach.[7]

The Critical Leader recognises that, when they bring kindness and integrity to the workplace, they are bringing energy to the Vital Connections. People want to work with them, and they provide the conditions and environment for people to do their best. The values of kindness, dignity and respect bring happiness with them. Surely when we are building organisations we should be heeding the advice of one man, Elwood P. Dowd who, with his pooka (imaginary rabbit) said, 'I always have a wonderful time, wherever I am, whomever I'm with.'[8]

Having fun

Managers and others on the path to Critical Leadership and organisational transformation must lose their job titles and say 'Good morning' when they arrive at work; they must recognise themselves and their colleagues as people bringing gifts and even genius to work; they must set minimum critical specifications and then allow people the room to do the work that has to be done.

The work of the Critical Leader is to help people to do what they cannot do by themselves. Our starting point, the need to see our organisations differently, is also our conclusion. We do not like a lot of what we have seen in organisations. They could be happier and more successful. We should be having fun at work but it seems that few know how to do that in this new and rather daunting era. Critical Leaders can do it; they can transform the nature of work to help their people to be the best they can be in a fulfilling workplace, as they help their organisations to adapt and grow. They can develop a workplace full of sparks of energy flowing between the Vital Connections.

Our final words come from Anita Roddick's Body Shop — a remarkable, and now legendary, success story which demonstrated to a jaded world that an inspirational, caring, responsible and profitable approach to business is within reach of all those who have the imagination and courage to try.

The Body Shop

The Body Shop's business practices are defined by our core values: care for the environment, concern for human rights and opposition to the exploitation of animals.

Through regular reviews and assessments of our operations around the world, we set ourselves clear targets to achieve best environmental practice—and time scales within which to meet those targets.

Energy

From one shop in Brighton in 1976 to over 1100 in 45 countries today, The Body Shop has rarely taken a decision without considering the environmental and social implications.

We do not sell products which consume a disproportionate amount of energy during manufacture or disposal, we do not generate excessive wastes, use ingredients from threatened habitats, or adversely affect other cultures or environments.

The future planning of our business will be guided as much by the environmental implications of our business as by economics.

Mission statement—our reason for being
To dedicate our business to the pursuit of social and environmental change.

To *Creatively* balance the financial and human needs of our stakeholders: employees, customers, franchisees, suppliers and shareholders.

To *Courageously* ensure that our business is ecologically sustainable: meeting the needs of the present without compromising the future.

To *Meaningfully* contribute to local, national and international communities in which we trade, by adopting a code of conduct which ensures care, honesty, fairness and respect.

To *Passionately* campaign for the protection of the environment, human and civil rights and to campaign against animal testing within the cosmetics and toiletries industry.

To *Tirelessly* work to narrow the gap between principle and practice, whilst making fun, passion and care part of our daily lives.

Source: The Body Shop Fact Sheets: 'Environmental Management' and 'The Business of The Body Shop'.

Discovery

Energy

The machine	*The garden*
The organisation does whatever it takes to make a profit	The organisation makes a profit without sacrificing an ethical approach
People are paid for their work	People are treated with dignity, respect and kindness, as well as being paid fairly
People are paid to do what they are told without feeling valued	People are encouraged to contribute ideas and energy in all areas
Many conflicting messages about values emerge through the conflict between talk and action	The organisation practises integrity before they talk about it
Executives are paid more to shoulder the burden of responsibility	Responsibility for the organisation rests with everyone
Management has a duty to the shareholders	Leaders have a philosophy, a set of high standards which they enact and communicate to customers, shareholders and colleagues

Appendix: Leadership

It is through educational awareness supported by continuous learning that organisations discover the power they have to make the leap towards an adaptive future. Learning must cover the critical aspects of leadership. This is the only way to actually make a difference in your organisation.

This appendix explores some of the models of leadership that preceded the concept of the Critical Leader. These models, although not incorporated directly in this work, have provided the knowledge and learning that brought all of us to our current understanding. It is from the ideas and experiences of these thinkers that this book has jumped in search of new meaning. By leveraging a wide base of learning, we may find a future in which leadership has squarely taken its place, and people are respected for who they are.

The main issues for leaders

Leadership has always been concerned with many varied issues. The most important include:

- effectiveness
- morale
- communication
- innovation
- systems
- future-thinking
- decision-making
- keeping good people.

Effectiveness

This is primarily the concern of turning paperwork generated from the strategic planning session, where it looked great, to the task of involving the people of the organisation in the implementation and success of the strategic plan.

Morale

Organisations are nothing more than groups of people joined together to accomplish tasks that are too great for individuals. Leaders must be concerned with creating and maintaining high morale among their teams. If the morale is low, an organisation will never be effective.

Communication

The fact that an organisation consists of people demands that the people be both free to speak and be heard. People do not appreciate the organisation, its goals and problems, unless they feel that they are listened to and are contributing in a meaningful way to its accomplishments. It is the task of a leader to ensure that communication is open. This is one of the most difficult functions of leaders, and perhaps also the least understood. The leader of a large organisation was once questioned as to how he knew that the agreed-upon strategic plan would be wholeheartedly adopted by the troops in the trenches. His response was that he was quite sure that the troops had bought into the strategy, because his direct reports said so.

Innovation

Organisational survival demands continuous innovation. However, too often innovation is approached as if it may be simply demanded or asked for, and the 'workers' will comply. As a job requirement, as part of a duty statement, innovation will never truly occur. Leaders must be prepared to provide the vision and direction that will unleash the potential of their people.

Systems

New organisations incorporate more technology in their various processes than in the past. The entire concept of how an organisation 'hangs together' is being transformed. Leaders need to rethink the sociology of business and figure out how people fit into a systems-driven world.

Future-thinking

The current environment has bred a culture that is focused on the extreme short term. While a short-term focus may occasionally be necessary, the organisation that will prosper in the future must have leaders who learn how to plan and think in future terms, so that it is adaptive, providing for the long run.

Decision-making

Leaders need to develop the confidence to allow significant decisions to be made at lower levels within the organisation. This is required so that the organisation develops the flexibility it needs to remain effective in the changing environment. It means a shifting of some decision-making power from people with titles to 'the right people with the right capabilities' to effect these decisions.

Keeping good people

It is impossible to have an organisation function effectively without the assistance of motivated people who are focused as a group. Good people are the foundations of all organisations. One of the key objectives of organisational leaders must be to encourage them to stay.

| Appendix: Leadership |

Key leadership theories

There has been much 'science' applied in many of the traditional approaches to the question of what makes an effective leader. Many researchers have searched for the answer to the 'leadership question'—many continue to look. The major categories under which the leadership question has been tackled include:

- trait theories
- behaviour and style theories
- situational and contingency theories.

These theories are explored briefly below. All the theories have a certain amount of validity. Yet, they have all failed to fully explain the differences between effective and ineffective leadership. Further, attempting to box aspects of leadership or tasks of the leader has the effect of separation: the people become distanced from the organisation; the present becomes disconnected from the future; the leader stands apart from the people and the customers.

While all perhaps were appropriate to the thinking of the time, in today's fast-changing environment of organisational quakes, these theories seem to miss the mark. As emphasised throughout *Roses and Rust*, to pursue the mark one must perceive the organisation anew, acknowledging that leadership, rather than management, is the necessary key to survival in the chaotic times ahead. It is also mandatory that the relationship between the Critical Leader and the organisation's Vital Connections be developed and strengthened, focusing on organisational survival.

Trait theories

Trait theory was the first real theory of leadership. Trait theories state that if the identifying characteristics—or traits—of leaders can be found, then the leadership problem may be solved. These theories also say that effective leaders cannot be made (that is, trained)—they are born.

Appendix: Leadership

Therefore, all one has to do is identify the right traits and then select people with those traits for leadership positions. Some of the 'effective leader' traits identified by researchers in studies before 1950 included:[1]

- intelligence that is above average but not genius level
- ability to solve complex abstract problems
- initiative, independence and inventiveness
- capacity to perceive a need for action and the will to do it
- self-assurance.

Some studies also mention the presence of enthusiasm, sociability, integrity, courage, imagination, decisiveness, determination and energy as general characteristics of effective leaders.

More recent studies have added a new trait—the helicopter factor. This is the ability to rise above the particulars of a situation and perceive it in relation to the overall environment.

However, even though many hundreds of studies have been conducted, there has been a failure to isolate traits that consistently and universally distinguish leaders from followers or that distinguish ineffective from effective leaders. Further criticisms of trait theories include:

- possession of all the traits is impossible
- there are too many exceptions
- the traits are at best necessary but not sufficient conditions for effectiveness
- traits are too ill-defined to be useful in practice.

Trait theory has therefore not proved particularly useful in enhancing our understanding of what makes an effective leader.

Behaviour and style theories

When flaws began appearing in trait theory, researchers began to look at the *behaviour* of leaders—what they 'did' (for example, how they communicated with team members or delegated tasks), rather than what they were born with. Behaviour theory had the advantage that as behaviours can be learned, leaders can be trained in effectiveness.

Like trait theory, however, research failed to find behaviours that were consistently applied across all situations. It was this finding that led to the emergence of the situational or contingency theories, discussed below.

Some researchers did, however, conclude that certain behaviours are effective across a wide range of situations. These researchers have since focused on various aspects of leadership behaviour, one of which is leadership *style*.

Researchers found two main leadership styles—the first focused on the task, while the second focused on employees. Task-oriented leaders closely supervise employees, while employee-oriented leaders try to motivate rather than control employees. There is evidence that an employee-oriented leadership style:

- improves team member satisfaction
- leads to lower turnover and grievance rates
- results in less inter-group conflict.

However, researchers have had difficulty in quantifying the benefits of the 'style' approach to leadership. All of the research findings also suggest that style alone is not the answer to effective leadership, although there does appear to be some evidence suggesting that a supportive or employee-oriented style of leadership leads to a higher degree of contentment and to a greater involvement of the work group. As with trait theory, the research into leadership style revealed that no style was effective in all situations (for example, influencing factors included the type of task, the organisational climate, and managerial values and experience). The next logical step was to identify the *situations* that were appropriate to a particular leadership style.

Leadership style theories are not inconsistent with our model of Critical Leadership. We believe that style is vital for leadership effectiveness. It is one of the separating aspects from management. And, there are certainly particular behaviours that are more effective in a climate of organisational quakes—and it is these behaviours that have been explored throughout *Roses and Rust*.

Situational and contingency theories

There is something to be gained from each of the situational leadership models, which say that the style of leadership must be modified to deal with changing situations. Situational leadership theories identify the various factors that are believed to influence leadership behaviour, while contingency theories attempt to identify which factors are most important in any given set of circumstances.

However, in general it is dangerous to adopt the situational and contingency models in the current environment. They suggest, to us, that attainment of a status quo is the desired end of leadership. They suggest the possibility of pre-programming in order to achieve leadership effectiveness. But now and in the future the leader must more and more rely on wits than on theoretical models.

Research into leadership theory became more systematic once the importance of the situation was considered. It was then that the leadership 'models' began to appear. There are four situational or contingency leadership approaches that are useful to explore when trying to define effective leadership. They are:

- the life-cycle approach
- Fielder's leadership style continuum
- the Vroom–Yetton model
- path–goal theory.

These models try to pinpoint the patterns in various situations that are important for effective leadership. However, it is difficult for any one person to adapt to many different styles dependent on the situation. In exploring these leadership models, it is beneficial to consider what type of leader may be the most effective in a given situation, but it is doubtful that one leader could actually accomplish this.

Appendix: Leadership

The life-cycle approach

Paul Hersey's and Kenneth H. Blanchard's life-cycle theory states that the level of the maturity of the team members affects the involvement required of the leader. The more mature the team members, the less direct involvement required. The theory defines maturity as:

- the desire for achievement
- the willingness and ability to take responsibility
- task-relevant ability
- task-relevant experience.

The life-cycle theory suggests that leader behaviour must change as the maturity of team members increases. Advocates of the theory make the assumption that employees are increasingly becoming more educated, motivated and technically competent. This provides for greater opportunities in terms of self-direction and self-control. This assumption also supports the movement towards the new type of organisation, which is more loosely structured, and the virtual corporation. These new approaches to how work gets done can only be effective with a mature workforce. While this theory is not fully researched, there are ample conceptual issues that support the usefulness of this theory.

Fielder's leadership style continuum

Fielder in *A Theory of Leadership Effectiveness*[2] developed a continuum of leadership styles that considers both the situation and the leader's style or personality. Questions Fielder considered were:

- To what degree does the situation provide the leader with the power and influence needed to be effective?
- How much can the effects of leadership style be predicted in terms of the behaviour of team members?

Fielder's model suggests that there are three factors that will impact on the effectiveness of a leader. These are:

Appendix: Leadership

- leader–member relations
- task structure
- position power.

A group may be classified with these factors. The argument suggests that it is easier to lead in a situation where the leader has a strong power position, where the work situation has a high task structure and where good leader–member relations exist.

Advocates of this contingency model have studied leaders ranging from the military to education to industrial fields, although one of the criticisms of the theory is that only a limited number of unusual groups have been studied.

If it is true, however, that effective leadership is based upon the combination of style and situation, then to create effective leadership, other than changing the leader, the leader's personality, motivational techniques or situation must change. Fielder comments on the difficulty of training leaders:

Fitting the man to the leadership job by selection and training has not been spectacularly successful. It is surely easier to change almost anything in the job situation than a man's personality and his leadership style.[3]

Fielder's approach to the leadership problem is useful because it reminds us that there are occasions when it pays to be distant and task centred rather than democratic. Fielder's research reveals that a leader's performance depends on both personality and situational favourableness. Fielder contends that training programs and experience can improve a leader's power and influence, but only if situational favourableness is already high. One possible conclusion is that a training program that is targeted to improve power and influence will be effective when it is for a relationship-oriented person. However, that same program may be detrimental for the task-oriented person.

An important conclusion from the work of Fielder is that it brought into being the ability to analyse situations from a leadership perspective,

Appendix: Leadership

and to begin to understand the importance of changing situations in order to increase leadership effectiveness.

The Vroom–Yetton model

This model was developed from research that suggested the autocratic approach to leadership was not the most effective. Effectiveness increased if team members were permitted to participate more in the decision-making process. Victor H. Vroom and Philip Yetton created a model that shows when participative decision-making is effective.[4] A number of assumptions were made in their decision-making model.

These include:

- The model should be of value in deciding the appropriate style of leadership for different types of situations.
- There is no one universal leadership style that is effective in all situations.
- The style used in one situation should not limit the style used in others.
- The focus should be first on the problem to be solved, and then on the environment/situation in which the problem occurs.

The Vroom–Yetton model focused upon two criteria of effectiveness: quality and acceptance. Quality relates to decisions that impact performance. Acceptance, which is often not considered in the decision-making process by leaders, deals with the team members buying in to the decision that is made. Many decisions fail, and leaders are unsuccessful, because they fail to understand the importance of receiving acceptance of their decision by their team members.

However, not all problems require buy-in in terms of decision-making. This again brings in the situational judgment that is dealt with in the Vroom–Yetton model. In deciding how much and when team members should participate in the decision-making process, two key assumptions should be considered.

Appendix: Leadership

- Will the people have to execute the decision, and does this occur in an environment where the people will need to apply initiative and judgment?
- Will the people feel strongly about the decision being made?

In these types of situations the leadership style chosen must aim to create an atmosphere where the people feel as though the decision being made is their own.

Vroom and Yetton have suggested that there are five leadership styles that may be applied in deciding the degree of participative decision-making. These include two autocratic approaches, two consultative approaches and a group approach.

This breaks the leadership problem into five leadership styles from which to choose, and the choice is based on the answer to seven questions: The five styles are:

AI: You solve the problem or make the decision yourself, using information available to you at the time.
AII: You obtain the necessary information from your team members, then decide on the solution to the problem yourself.
CI: You share the problem with the people individually, getting their ideas and suggestions, then you make the decision.
CII: You share the problem with your team members in a group, then you make the decision.
GII: You share the problem with the people as a group, then together you make the decision.

The seven questions, which are typically set out in a decision tree, are:

- Is one decision likely to be better than another? If not, then AI is the solution.
- Does the leader know enough to solve it on his or her own? If not, avoid AI.
- Is the problem clear cut and structured? If not, go to CII or GII.

Appendix: Leadership

- Must all the people accept this decision? If not, then AI and AII are possible.
- Would they accept your decision? If not, then GII is preferred.
- Do the people share your goals for the organisation? If not, then GII is risky.
- Are the people likely to conflict with each other? If yes, then CII is better.

The Vroom–Yetton model was a large step forward in looking at approaches to leadership style and effectiveness. However, the danger is that it can still provide an escape from judgment.

The path–goal model
Like other models that focus on situations, the path–goal model tries to predict how effective various styles of leadership will be in different situations. This model states that leaders are effective because they create:

- a positive impact on the team members' motivation to work
- an impact on the team members' ability to perform the work
- a provision of satisfaction for team members doing the work.

The path–goal theory focuses on the leader's ability to influence the team members' perception of work goals, self-development goals and paths to goal attainment.

The path–goal model is based on the expectancy motivation theory. This theory states that a person's attitudes, job satisfaction, behaviour and job effort are predictable from:

- the degree to which the job or behaviour is seen as leading to various outcomes—that is, the expectancy of reward
- the preferences for these outcomes—that is, how attractive is the reward (valence).

This means that people achieve job satisfaction if they believe that it leads somewhere, and they will work hard if they believe it will result in positive outcomes. This presents implications for the style approach to leadership. The path–goal model suggests that the leader's style must influence the expectancy and valence of team members.

Path–goal theory developed two propositions that were presented by House and Mitchell. These are:

Leader behaviour is acceptable and satisfying to the extent that the subordinates perceive such behaviour as an immediate source of satisfaction or as instrumental to future satisfaction.[5]

Leader behaviour will be motivational to the extent that it makes satisfaction of subordinates' needs contingent on effective performance and it complements the environment of subordinates by providing the guidance, clarity of direction and rewards necessary for effective performance.[6]

Path–goal theorists have identified two contingency variables that help determine the most effective leadership style. These are:

- the personal characteristics of team members
- the environmental pressures and demands in the workplace.

For example, if team members have a high perceived ability relative to the task (a personal characteristic), the less they will accept a directive type of leader.

Environmental pressures and demands (for example, how structured the task is) include factors that are not controllable by the team members, but nevertheless are important variables that impact the team members' ability to effectively do the job, or receive satisfaction from doing the job.

Path–goal theory suggests that leader behaviour is motivational to the extent that it assists the team members in dealing with environmental factors. For example, if a leader is able to eliminate some of the volatility in the environment, then the team member is motivated to believe that the job is that much more accomplishable.

Appendix: Leadership

The path-goal theory took Fielder's model further by not only suggesting the types of leadership style that are effective in certain situations, but also by attempting to say why they are effective.

Towards new models of leadership

A person may be appointed to a high position but never to leadership.

Charles Handy[7]

Leadership in the self-renewing and thriving enterprise is characterised by its willingness to move beyond tidy models of what leadership is and does. Leaders establish order and discipline, and simultaneously foster scepticism, incredulity, experimentation, and change. They encourage the generation of new forms and actions that may have neither precedent nor accustomed approval. They inject creative enzymes into the system, with results that can be destabilising and disorderly and are rarely parametric. They know that to achieve more and better results, more resourcefulness is as important as more resources.

Mukhi, Hampton and Barnwell[8]

Clearly there is no one model of leadership that is universally appropriate. Most organisations do not have leaders who are totally supportive of one style or another. However, there are a number of important variables that must be taken into account in order to obtain a minimum level of leadership effectiveness. For example, Gibson, Ivancevich and Donnelly[9] have suggested the following variables:

- the leader's awareness of self
- group characteristics
- understanding individual characteristics

Appendix: Leadership

- understanding motivation
- situational variables.

Leadership is perhaps the most studied and the least understood of all management functions. In fact, several writings in the field have relayed apparent frustration at the lack of clear understanding that comes out of all the research. Part of this problem stems from the lack of a clear definition of what anyone means by leadership. However, today, there appear to be two basic definitions of leadership applied to the problems of managing organisations.

One is the Big Picture. This defines leadership as the function of defining, building and maintaining an organisation's distinctive character and culture. The other defines leadership as the interpersonal process by which leaders influence team members to accomplish certain tasks.

Peters and Waterman in their study of excellent companies state:

How did these companies get where they are? Is it always a case of a strong leader at the helm? We must admit that our bias at the beginning was to discount the role of leadership heavily, if for no other reason than that everybody's answer to what's wrong (or right) with whatever organisation is its leader. Our strong belief was that the excellent companies have gotten to be the way they are because of a unique set of cultural attributes that distinguish them from the rest, and if we understood those attributes well enough, we could do more than just mutter 'leadership' in response to questions like 'Why is J&J (Johnson and Johnson) so good?' Unfortunately what we found was that associated with almost every excellent company was a strong leader (or two) who seemed to have a lot to do with making the company excellent in the first place.[10]

It is through understanding of past quests to understand the leadership question that we can begin to explore the future, coming to an understanding of what is required by us in terms of leadership to survive and prosper.

Appendix: Leadership

The work of Kouzes and Posner, referred to throughout *Roses and Rust*, has moved us a long way forward. This work does not seek to constrain what is meant by leadership. It asks us what it is we need. And we have answered. *Roses and Rust* has focused on the Critical Leader in an environment of transformational quakes. It begs for empathy with the people of organisations. We believe it defines the key aspect of leadership required today. That is—to help! Critical Leaders help the organisation to adapt and grow, and they help their people to be the best that they can be. Critical Leadership answers the question: What are leaders, throughout the organisation, to do? What is its purpose? The work of Kouzes and Posner tells us then how the Critical Leader is to work.

Organisations must become places that are fit for our children to work. They must earn their place and their future through caring for their people and their customers.

It is the work of Critical Leaders to create such organisations.

> *The future ain't what it used to be.*
> *Yogi Berra*
>
> *Oh good, nobody here but people.*
> *Mrs Veta Simmons*, Harvey

Endnotes

Chapter 1

1. Ian I. Mitroff and Harold A. Linstone (1993) *The Unbounded Mind: Breaking the Chains of Traditional Business Thinking*, New York: Oxford University Press, p. 142.
2. Ibid.
3. Oliver Sacks (1995) *An Anthropologist on Mars*, London: Picador, p. 115.
4. Dr Deepak Chopra, among others, has written about the 'process' that is our body. A good starting point if you wish to read further is Chopra's book (1989) *Quantum Healing: Exploring the Frontiers of the Mind/Body Medicine*, New York: Bantam.
5. Sacks, op. cit., p. xiv.
6. Ibid., p. xiii.
7. Brian Goodwin (1994) *How the Leopard Changed Its Spots*, London: Weidenfeld & Nicolson, p. 65.
8. Ibid., p. 66.

Chapter 2

1. The concept of 'Thank God it's Monday' is from Alfie Kohn (1993) *Punished by Rewards*, New York: Houghton Mifflin.
2. Margaret Wheatley (1992) *Leadership and the New Science*, San Francisco: Berrett-Koehler, p. 52.
3. Peter F. Drucker (1992) *Managing for the Future: The 1990s and Beyond*, New York: Truman Talley, p. 119.
4. As sourced in Marvin Weisbord (1987) *Productive Workplaces: Organizing and Managing for Dignity, Meaning and Community*, San Francisco: Jossey-Bass, p. 326.
5. (1991) 'Service Training Made Simple', in *Training and Development Journal*, January, pp. 37–8.
6. James M. Kouzes and Barry Z. Posner (1987) *The Leadership Challenge*, San Francisco: Jossey-Bass, p. 146.
7. Gary Hamel and C. K. Prahalad (1994) *Competing for the Future*, Boston: Harvard Business School Press, p. 135.
8. Kohn, op. cit., pp. 189–90.
9. Quoted by David Limerick and Bert Cunnington (1993) in *Managing the New Organisation*, Sydney: Business & Professional Publishing, p. 1.
10. Wheatley, op. cit., p. 191.

Endnotes

11. Ralph Kilmann as reported in John P. Kotter and James L. Heskett (1992) *Corporate Culture and Performance*, New York: Free Press, pp. 44–5.
12. Warren Bennis (1993) *An Invented Life*, London: Century, p. 57.
13. Oliver Sacks (1985) *The Man Who Mistook His Wife for a Hat*, London: Pan, p. 2.
14. Ned Herrmann (1989) *The Creative Brain*, Lake Lure: Brain Books.
15. Max De Pree (1989) *Leadership is an Art*, Melbourne: Australian Business Library, pp. 7–8.
16. Jack Welch as quoted in Noel M. Tichy and Stratford Sherman (1993) *Control your Destiny or Someone Else Will*, New York: Doubleday, p. 246.
17. Hamel and Prahalad, op cit.
18. 'Your Company's Most Valuable Asset: Intellectual Capital' (1994) *Fortune*, 3 October.

Chapter 3

1. M. Scott Peck (1993) *A World Waiting to be Born: Civility Rediscovered*, New York: Bantam, p. 33.
2. John P. Kotter and James L. Heskett (1992) *Corporate Culture and Performance*, New York: Free Press.
3. Ibid., p. 59.
4. Research quoted in Alfie Kohn (1993) *Punished by Rewards*, New York: Houghton Mifflin, p. 69.
5. Sir Charles Sherrington was a pioneer in neurophysiology. This is excerpted from Tony Buzan (1993) *The Mind Map Book*, London: BBC, p. 26.
6. Jan Carlzon (1987) *Moments of Truth*, Sydney: Harper & Row, p. 3.
7. Ibid., from the introduction.
8. Scott Peck, op. cit., p. 276.
9. Murray Gell-Mann (1994) *The Quark and the Jaguar: Adventures in the Simple and the Complex*, London: Little, Brown & Company, p. 25.
10. T. J. Cartwright, in Margaret Wheatley (1992) *Leadership and the New Science*, San Francisco: Berrett-Koehler, p. 123.
11. Refer to Gary Hamel and C. K. Prahalad (1994) *Competing for the Future*, Boston: Harvard Business School Press, and Chapter 1.
12. Marvin Weisbord (1987) *Productive Workplaces: Organizing and Managing for Dignity, Meaning and Community*, San Francisco: Jossey-Bass, p. 73.
13. Staff of Zenger-Miller, Inc., 'Training for Organisational Excellence', *Canberra Bulletin of Public Administration*, Vol. 14(4), pp. 135–42.
14. Peter F. Drucker (1992) *Managing for the Future: The 1990s and Beyond*, New York: Truman Talley, pp. 193–4.
15. John Kotter (1982) 'The General Managers', *Harvard Business Review*, December.
16. Carlzon, op. cit., p. 88 and p. 38.
17. Quoted by David Limerick and Bert Cunnington (1993) in *Managing the New Organisation*, Sydney: Business & Professional Publishing, p. 1.

Endnotes

Chapter 4

1. Mihaly Csikszentmihalyi (1992) *Flow: The Psychology of Happiness*, London: Rider, pp. 216–17. This book was published in the US under the title *Flow: The Psychology of Optimal Experience*.
2. James M. Kouzes and Barry Z. Posner (1987) *The Leadership Challenge*, San Francisco: Jossey-Bass, p. xxi.
3. From *Harvey*, the movie.
4. As quoted in H. Woodward and S. Bucholtz (1987) *Aftershock: Helping People Through Corporate Change*, New York: John Wiley & Sons, p. 57.
5. Ibid., p. 87.
6. T. Gross, R. T. Pascales and A. G. Athos (1993) 'The Reinvention Roller Coaster: Risking the Present for a Powerful Future', *Harvard Business Review*, November–December.
7. Ibid.
8. M. Scott-Peck (1993) *A World Waiting to be Born: Civility Rediscovered*, New York: Bantam, p. 276.
9. James M. Kouzes and Barry Z. Posner (1993) *Credibility: How Leaders Gain and Lose It, Why People Demand It*, San Francisco: Jossey-Bass, p. 125.
10. Kouzes and Posner (1987) op. cit.
11. J. Duck (1993) 'Managing Change: The Art of Balancing', *Harvard Business Review*, November–December.

Chapter 5

1. David Limerick and Bert Cunnington (1993) *Managing the New Organisation*, Sydney: Business & Professional Publishing, p. 212.
2. Stephen R. Covey, A. Roger Merrill and Rebecca R. Merrill (1994) *First Things First*, New York: Simon & Schuster, pp. 88–9.
3. Margaret Wheatley (1992) *Leadership and the New Science: Learning About Organisation From an Orderly Universe*, San Francisco: Berrett-Koehler, p. 76.
4. Ibid.
5. Ibid.
6. Ibid., p. 78.
7. Bennis and Nanus, quoted in James M. Kouzes and Barry Z. Posner (1987) *The Leadership Challenge*, San Francisco: Jossey-Bass, p. 84.
8. Ibid., p. 83.
9. Limerick and Cunnington, op. cit., p. 213.
10. Ibid., p. 224.
11. Ibid., p. 123.
12. Wheatley, op. cit., pp. 77–8.
13. Limerick and Cunnington, op. cit., p. 114.
14. Ibid., p. 119.

Endnotes

Chapter 6

1. As quoted in M. Gell-Mann (1994) *The Quark and the Jaguar: Adventures in the Simple and the Complex*, London: Little, Brown & Company, p. 11
2. Ibid., p. 10.
3. Peter Senge (1990) *The Fifth Discipline: The Art and Practice of the Learning Organization*, Sydney: Random House.
4. Gell-Mann, op. cit., p. 25
5. Ibid., p. 17.

Chapter 7

1. Thomas L. Quick (1993) *Unconventional Wisdom: Irreverent Solutions for Tough Problems at Work*, San Francisco: Jossey-Bass, pp. 97–8.
2. Margaret Wheatley (1992) *Leadership and the New Science*, San Francisco: Berrett-Koehler, p. 7.
3. Nicholas Imparato and Oren Harari (1994) *Jumping the Curve*, San Francisco: Jossey-Bass, p. 119.
4. Ian I. Mitroff and Harold A. Linstone (1993) *The Unbounded Mind: Breaking the Chains of Traditional Business Thinking*, New York: Oxford University Press, p. 99.
5. Ibid., p. 101.
6. Jock Macneish and Tony Richardson (1994) *The Choice: Either Change the System or Polish the Fruit*, 2nd edition, Sydney: Don't Press, p. 22.
7. John Gribbin (1984) *In Search of Schroedinger's Cat: Quantum Physics and Reality*, London: Penguin, p. 205.
8. Robert J. Kriegel and Louis Patler (1992) *If It Ain't Broke—Break It*, Melbourne: Australian Business Library, p. 244.

Chapter 8

1. Marvin R. Weisbord (1987) *Productive Workplaces: Organizing and Managing for Dignity, Meaning and Community*, San Francisco: Jossey-Bass, p. 110.
2. We refer the reader to Jerry B. Harvey (1988) *The Abilene Paradox and Other Mediations on Management*, New York: Lexington.
3. Hugh Mackay (1993) *Reinventing Australia: The Mind and Mood of Australia in the 90s*, Sydney: Angus & Robertson, p. 265.
4. Kathleen Eisenhardt, in Tom Peters (1992) *Liberation Management*, London: Macmillan, p. 42.
5. (1993) 'How Bell Labs Creates Star Perfomers', *Harvard Business Review*, July–August, p. 133.
6. M. Scott Peck (1993) *A World Waiting to be Born: Civility Rediscovered*, New York: Bantam.

Endnotes

7. Gary Hamel and C. K. Prahalad (1994) *Competing for the Future*, Boston: Harvard Business School Press, p. 61.
8. James C. Collins and Jerry I. Porras (1995) *Built to Last: Successful Habits of Visionary Companies*, London: Century, p. 150.
9. Ibid., pp. 152–3.
10. (1995) 'Ten Commandments for Managing Creative People', *Fortune*, 16 January.
11. (1994) 'And the Winner is Still . . . Wal-Mart', *Fortune*, 2 May.
12. Weisbord, op. cit., p. 273.
13. Nicholas Imparato and Oren Harari (1994) *Jumping the Curve*, San Francisco: Jossey-Bass, pp. 117–19.

Chapter 9

1. Max De Pree (1989) *Leadership is an Art*, Melbourne: Australian Business Library, p. 10.
2. Marvin Weisbord (1987) *Productive Workplaces: Organizing and Managing for Dignity, Meaning and Community*, San Francisco: Jossey-Bass, p. 279.
3. John P. Kotter and James L. Heskett (1992) *Corporate Culture and Performance*, New York: Free Press, p. 59.
4. T. J. Larkin (1987) 'Communicating Customer Service', Institute of Personal Management Australia.
5. (1995) 'Are You Being Served?', *The Sunday Herald*, 29 January.
6. (1994) 'Why Some Customers are More Equal than Others', *Fortune*, 19 September.
7. Noel M. Tichy and Stratford Sherman (1993) *Control Your Destiny or Someone Else Will*, New York: Doubleday, p. 8.
8. Gary Hamel and C. K. Prahalad (1994) *Competing for the Future*, Boston: Harvard Business School Press, pp. 203–4.
9. (1993) 'Succeeding with Tough Love', *Fortune*, 29 November.
10. A. Parasuraman, Valarie Zeithaml and Leonard L. Berry (1986) 'Servqual: A Multiple-Item Scale for Measuring Customer Perceptions of Service Quality', Working Paper of the Marketing Science Institute Research Program, Cambridge, Mass. We refer the reader to an introduction to these dimensions in Tom Peters (1992) *Liberation Management*, London: Macmillan, pp. 715–16, and Leonard L. Berry, David R. Bennett and Carter W. Brown (1989) *Service Quality: A Profit Strategy for Financial Institutions*, Illinois: Dow Jones-Irwin.
11. Kotter and Heskett, ibid.
12. Nicholas Imparato and Oren Harari (1994) *Jumping the Curve*, San Francisco: Jossey-Bass
13. The terms 'competence' and 'commitment' could be substituted from Ken Blanchard's *Situational Leadership* model. The performance equation of Imparato and Harari does not limit the effectiveness of the Situational Leadership model which remains an invaluable tool for making decisions about people based upon perceptions of their competence and commitment. This is a necessary job in itself.

Endnotes

[14] Imparato and Harari, op. cit., p. 68.
[15] Tichy and Sherman, op. cit., p. 231.
[16] Imparato and Harari, op. cit., p. 60.
[17] We refer the reader to Alfie Kohn's book (1993) *Punished by Rewards: The Trouble with Gold Stars, Incentive Plans, A's, Praise and Other Bribes*, New York: Houghton Mifflin.
[18] Ibid., p. 69.
[19] Ibid., p. 181, based on the work of Douglas McGregor.
[20] Hamel and Prahalad, op. cit., p. 135.
[21] As reported in Richard Tanner Pascale (1990) *Managing on the Edge: How the Smartest Companies Use Conflict to Stay Ahead*, New York: Touchstone, p. 250.
[22] This material is from (1995) 'Ten Commandments for Managing Creative People', *Fortune*, 16 January. Another illuminating account of the 3M company appears in James C. Collins and Jerry I. Porras (1995) *Built to Last: Successful Habits of Visionary Companies*, London: Century.
[23] Ibid.
[24] Ibid.
[25] Peter Block (1990) *The Empowered Manager: Positive Political Skills at Work*, San Francisco: Jossey-Bass, p. 91.

Chapter 10

[1] Max De Pree (1989) *Leadership is an Art*, Melbourne: Australian Business Library, p. 9.
[2] Alfred Adler (1931) *What Life Could Mean To You*, Oxford: One World Publications, p. 16.
[3] Ibid, p. 18.
[4] Simon Longstaff (executive director of the St James Ethics Centre) (1995) 'Carrot and a Stick for Bold Riders', *Australian Business Monthly*, March.
[5] Peter Block (1993) *Stewardship: Choosing Service Over Self-Interest*, San Francisco: Berrett-Koehler, pp. 165–6.
[6] As we have elsewhere, we refer the reader to the work of Stephen Covey, Peter Block, Alfie Kohn and James Kouzes and Barry Posner. Their books are listed in the bibliography.
[7] James M. Kouzes and Barry Z. Posner (1987) *The Leadership Challenge*, San Francisco: Jossey-Bass, p. 187.
[8] From the movie *Harvey*, with James Stewart playing Elwood P. Dowd and Harvey as himself.

Appendix

[1] C. B. Handy (1993) *Understanding Organizations*, 4th edn, London: Penguin.
[2] F. E. Fielder (1967) *A Theory of Leadership Effectiveness*, McGraw-Hill: New York.

Endnotes

3. F. E. Fielder (1965) 'Engineering the Job to Fit the Manager', *Harvard Business Review*, September–October, p. 115.
4. V. H. Vroom and P. Yetton (1973) *Leadership and Decision Making*, Pittsburgh: University of Pittsburgh Press.
5. R. H. House and T. R. Mitchell (1974) 'Path–Goal Theory of Leadership', *Journal of Contemporary Business*, Autumn, p. 84.
6. J. L. Gibson, J. M. Ivancevich and J. H. Donnelly Jr (1979) *Organizations: Behavior, Structure, Processes*, Dallas: Business Publications, p. 221.
7. Handy, ibid, p. 102.
8. S. Mukhi, D. Hampton and N. Barnwell (1990) *Australian Management*, McGraw-Hill, Sydney, p. 65.
9. Gibson, Ivancevich and Donnelly, op. cit..
10. T. J. Peters and R. H. Waterman Jr (1982) *In Search of Excellence: Lessons from America's Best-run Companies*, New York: Harper & Row, p. 26.

Bibliography

Books

Adler, Alfred (1931) *What Life Could Mean to You,* Oxford: One World Publication (republished 1992).

Bennis, Warren (1993) *An Invented Life: Reflections on Leadership and Change,* London: Century.

Berry, Leonard L., Bennett, David R. and Brown, Carter W. (1989) *Service Quality: A Profit Strategy for Financial Institutions,* Homewood, Ill: Dow Jones-Irwin.

Block, Peter (1990) *The Empowered Manager: Positive Political Skills at Work,* San Francisco: Jossey-Bass.

Block, Peter (1993) *Stewardship: Choosing Service Over Self-Interest,* San Francisco: Berrett-Koehler.

Buzan, Tony (1993) *The Mind Map Book,* London: BBC.

Carlzon, Jan (1987) *Moments of Truth,* Sydney: Harper & Row.

Chopra, Deepak (1989) *Quantum Healing: Exploring the Frontiers of Mind/Body Medicine,* New York: Bantam.

Collins, James C. and Porras, Jerry I. (1995) *Built to Last: Successful Habits of Visionary Companies,* London: Century.

Covey, Stephen R. (1989) *The Seven Habits of Highly Effective People: Restoring the Character Ethic,* New York, Simon & Schuster.

Covey, Stephen R. (1991) *Principle-Centred Leadership,* New York: Summit Books.

Covey, Stephen R., Merrill, A. Roger and Merrill, Rebecca R. (1994) *First Things First: To Live, to Love, to Learn, to Leave a Legacy,* New York: Simon & Schuster.

Csikszentmihalyi, Mihaly (1992) *Flow: The Psychology of Happiness,* London: Rider.

De Bono, Edward (1990) *Six Thinking Hats,* London: Penguin.

De Pree, Max (1989) *Leadership is an Art,* Melbourne: Australian Business Library.

Drucker, Peter F. (1969) *The Age of Discontinuity,* New York: Harper & Row.

Drucker, Peter F. (1974) *Management: Tasks, Responsibilities, Practices,* New York: Harper & Row.

Drucker, Peter F. (1980) *Managing in Turbulent Times,* New York: Harper & Row.

Drucker, Peter F. (1989) *The New Realities,* London: Mandarin.

Drucker, Peter F. (1992) *Managing for the Future: The 1990s and Beyond,* New York: Truman Talley.

Fulghum, Robert (1988) *All I Ever Really Need to Know I Learned in Kindergarten,* New York: Villard Books.

Gell-Mann, Murray (1994) *The Quark and the Jaguar: Adventures in the Simple and the Complex,* London: Little, Brown & Company.

Bibliography

Goodwin, Brian (1994) *How the Leopard Changed Its Spots*, London: Weidenfeld & Nicolson.
Gribbin, John (1984) *In Search of Schroedinger's Cat: Quantum Physics and Reality*, New York: Bantam.
Hamel, Gary and Prahalad, C. K. (1994) *Competing for the Future*, Boston: Harvard Business School Press.
Harvey, Jerry B. (1988) *The Abilene Paradox and Other Mediations on Management*, New York: Lexington.
Herrmann, Ned (1989) *The Creative Brain*, Lake Lure: Brain Books.
Hickman, C. R. and Silva, M. A. (1987) *The Future 500: Creating Tomorrow's Organizations Today*, New York: NAL Books.
Hilmer, Frederick G. (1989) *New Games, New Rules—Work in Competitive Enterprises*, Sydney: Angus & Robertson.
Imparato, Nicholas & Harari, Oren (1994) *Jumping the Curve: Innovation and Strategic Choice in an Age of Transition*, San Francisco: Jossey-Bass.
Kohn, Alfie (1993) *Punished by Rewards: The Trouble with Gold Stars, Incentive Plans, A's, Praise, and Other Bribes*, New York: Houghton Mifflin.
Kotter, John P. and Heskett, James L. (1992) *Corporate Culture and Performance*, New York: Free Press.
Kouzes, James M. and Posner, Barry Z. (1987) *The Leadership Challenge: How to Keep Getting Extraordinary Things Done in Organizations*, San Francisco: Jossey-Bass.
Kouzes, James M. and Posner, Barry Z. (1993) *Credibility: How Leaders Gain and Lose it, Why People Demand it*, San Francisco: Jossey-Bass.
Kriegel, Robert J. and Patler, Louis (1992) *If It Ain't Broke—Break It!*, Melbourne: Australian Business Library.
Larkin, T. J. (1987) 'Communicating Customer Service', Institute of Personal Management Australia.
Larkin, T. J. and Larkin, Sandar (1994) *Communicating Change: Winning Employee Support for New Business Goals*, New York: McGraw-Hill.
Limerick, David and Cunnington, Bert (1993) *Managing the New Organisation: A Blueprint for Networks and Strategic Alliances*, Sydney: Business & Professional Publishing.
Lippitt, C. (1982) *Organizational Renewal*, Englewood Cliffs, Prentice-Hall.
Mackay, Hugh (1993) *Reinventing Australia: The Mind and Mood of Australia in the 90s*, Sydney: Angus & Robertson.
Mitroff, Ian I. and Linstone, Harold A. (1993) *The Unbounded Mind: Breaking the Chains of Traditional Business Thinking*, New York: Oxford University Press.
Naisbitt, J. (1982) *Megatrends: Ten New Directions for Transforming Our Lives*, New York: Warner Books.
Pascale, Richard Tanner (1990) *Managing on the Edge: How the Smartest Companies Use Conflict to Stay Ahead*, New York: Touchstone.
Peck, M. Scott (1990) *The Different Drum: Community Building and Peace*, London: Arrow.
Peck, M. Scott (1993) *A World Waiting to be Born: Civility Rediscovered*, New York: Bantam.
Peters, Tom (1987) *Thriving On Chaos: Handbook for a Management Revolution*, New York: Knopf.

Bibliography

Peters, Tom (1992) *Liberation Management*, London: Macmillan.
Peters, Tom (1994) *The Tom Peters Seminar*, London: Macmillan.
Quick, Thomas L. (1993) *Unconventional Wisdom: Irreverent Solutions for Tough Problems at Work*, San Francisco: Jossey-Bass.
Report of the Industry Task Force on Leadership and Management Skills (1995) *Enterprising Nation: Renewing Australia's Managers to Meet the Challenges of the Asia-Pacific Century*, Canberra: Australian Government Publishing Service.
Sacks, Oliver (1995) *An Anthropologist on Mars*, London: Picador.
Sacks, Oliver (1985) *The Man Who Mistook His Wife for a Hat*, London: Pan.
Senge, Peter (1990) *The Fifth Discipline: The Art and Practice of the Learning Organization*, Sydney: Random House.
Tichy, Noel M. and Sherman, Stratford (1993) *Control Your Destiny or Someone Else Will*, New York: Doubleday.
Toffler, A. (1981) *The Third Wave*, London: Pan Books.
Vaill, Peter (1989) *Managing as a Performing Art*, San Francisco: Jossey-Bass.
Weisbord, Marvin R. (1987) *Productive Workplaces: Organizing and Managing for Dignity, Meaning and Community*, San Francisco: Jossey-Bass.
Weisbord, Marvin R. (1993) *Discovering Common Ground: How Future Search Conferences Bring People Together to Achieve Breakthrough Innovation, Empowerment, Shared Vision, and Collaborative Action*, San Francisco: Berrett-Koehler.
Wheatley, Margaret (1992) *Leadership and the New Science: Learning about Organization from an Orderly Universe*, San Francisco: Berrett-Koehler.
Woodward, H. and Bucholtz, S. (1987) *Aftershock: Helping People Through Corporate Change*, New York: John Wiley & Sons.

Articles

'And the Winner is Still . . . Wal-Mart', *Fortune*, 2 May 1994.
'Are You Being Served?', *The Sunday Herald-Sun*, 29 January 1995.
'Carrot and a Stick for Bold Riders', *Australian Business Monthly*, March 1995.
'David Glass Won't Crack Under Fire', *Fortune*, 8 February 1993.
Duck, J., 'Managing Change: The Art of Balancing', *Harvard Business Review*, November–December 1993.
Gross, T., Pascales, R.T. and Athos, A.G., 'The Reinvention Roller Coaster: Risking the Present for a Powerful Future', *Harvard Business Review*, November–December 1993.
Kotter, John, 'The General Managers', *Harvard Business Review*, December 1982.
Parasuraman A., Zeithaml, Valarie and Berry, Leonard L., 'Servqual: A Multiple-Item Scale for Measuring Customer Perceptions of Service Quality', Working Paper of the Marketing Science Institute Research Program, Cambridge, Mass., 1986.
'Service Training Made Simple', *Training and Development Journal*, January 1991.
Staff of Zenger-Miller, Inc., 'Training for Organisational Excellence', *Canberra Bulletin of Public Administration*, Vol. 14(4), pp. 135–42.
'Succeeding with Tough Love', *Fortune*, 29 November 1993.
'Why Some Customers are More Equal than Others', *Fortune*, 19 September 1994.
'Your Company's Most Valuable Asset: Intellectual Capital', *Fortune*, 3 October 1994.

Index

3M, 133, 134, 158, 159

Ability, *see* Performance
Accuracy of Role Perception (*ARP*), 147, 149, 157, 161
Adaptive cultures, 128, 129
Adaptive organisation, 47
Adaptive systems, xiii, 4–7, 8, 87, 105
Adler, Alfred, 166
Aftershock, 66
Agreement, 110
Ainsworth-Land, George, 33
Alignment, *see* Syzygy
All-Purpose Viewfinder, 111, 136
Analysis, 110
Ants, 6
ANZ, 47

Barnwell, N., 188
Behaviour theories, 178, 179–81
Behaviourists, xiv, 150, 151
Ben and Jerry's Ice Cream, 96
Bennis, Warren, 27
Best practices, 129, 151
Blanchard, H., 151, 182
Block, Peter, 169
Body Shop, The, 58, 167, 172–3
Boundaries, 21, 48
Brain, 5, 27, 43
Bucholtz, S., 66

Carlzon, Jan, 44, 59
Challenging the process, 62, 120
Change
 critical mass, 49, 55–8
 prescriptive approach, 49–54
 transformational leader, 49, 58–9
Chaos, 48
Chopra, Deepak, 4
Collins, James C., 133
Communication, 66, 67, 68, 69, 80, 116, 160, 176
Community, xiv, 46, 47, 54, 68, 88, 132, 158, 160
Complex, 92, 98, 102
Conflict, 110
Connections, xvii, 15, 40, 49, 91–107, *see also* Vital Connections
Contingency theories, 178, 181–8
Core competencies, 104, 144
Corporate immune system, 35, 49
Covey, Stephen, 74
Crisis, xi
Critical Leaders, 68, 75, 97, 86, 101, 102, 105, 121, 123, 125, 128, 129, 132, 133, 135, 140, 141, 145, 146, 148, 149, 152, 156, 158, 159, 163, 170, 171, 172,
Critical Leadership, xv, 9, 17–18, 19, 22, 40, 42, 89, 117
Critical Leadership model, xv, xvi
Csikszentmihalyi, Mihaly, 60
Cunnington, Bert, 66, 73, 79, 82, 83, 87
Customer service, 141, 142, 143, 134, 145, 161
 dimensions of, 145

Daily tasks, 122
De Bono, Edward, 135
De Pree, Max, 28, 139, 148, 164
Deciding, 128–38

Index

Decision-making, xvii, 47, 67, 128–37, 177
Decisions, 113
DeSimone, Livio, 134, 158
Dignity, 165
Directions, xvii, 73–90
Donelly, J. H., 188
Dowd, Elwood P., 171
Drucker, Peter, 18, 56, 57, 58

Economists, 130
Educationalists, 130
Effectiveness, 176
Einstein, Albert, 40
Employees, 8
Empowerment, 88
Energy, xix, 4, 163–74
Ethics, 163, 168
Evans, John, 114
Ewing, J. R., 167
Executives, 67
Experts, 31, 33, 130

False truths, 118, 120
Fear, 134–5
Fiedler, F. E., 182, 183
Footpaths, 84
Fun, 172
Future, *see* Preferred future
Future searches, 122
Future-thinking, 177

Garden organisation, *see* Organisations, garden
Gell-Mann, Murray, 48
General Electric, 24, 58, 59, 148
Gibson, J. L., 188
Glass, David, 59
Goals, 68, 73, 83
Gribbin, John, 117

Hamel, Gary, 23, 25, 32, 54, 133, 144, 152

Hampton, D., 188
Handy, Charles, 113, 188
Harari, Oren, 109, 136, 147, 149
Harvey, 171
Hay, Colonel, 96
Helping, xix, 139–62
Herman Miller, 28, 139
Herrmann, Ned, 27
Hersey, Paul, 182
Heskett, James, 41, 142, 146
Honda Motor Co. Ltd (US), 154

IBM, 129
Imparato, Nicholas, 109, 136, 147, 149
Incentive schemes, 151
Information, 22, 45, 69, 160
Innovation, 176
Insects, ants, 6
Integrity, 167
Intellectual capital, 15, 34
Interconnectiveness, 7
Ivancevich, J. M., 188

Job descriptions, 97

Kindergarten, 163
Knowing, 108–27, 109, 116, 117, 119
Knowledge, 113, 121
Kohn, Alfie, 23, 43, 97, 114, 151, 152
Kotter John, 41, 54, 58, 142, 146
Kouzes, James M., 62, 68, 120, 171,
Kriegel, Robert, 118

Larkin, T. J., 142, 143, 148
Leaders, 58, 91
Leadership, *see* Critical Leadership
Leadership, models of, 175–88
Leadership practices (Kouzes and Posner), 62, 69, 79
Learning, 26, 57, 87, 98, 101, 132, 133
Learning organisation, 102
Lewin, Kurt, 54, 55
Life-cycle approach, 182

202.

Index

Limerick, David, 66, 73, 79, 82, 83, 87
Linstone, Harold, 1, 109
Living systems, *see* Adaptive systems
Longstaff, Simon, 168

Macneish, Jock, 113
Manage by tinkering, 126
Management, xii, xiv, 1, 11, 17–18, 19, 39, 48, 108, 140, 153, 166
Manager, 156
Matsushita, 34
McGregor, Douglas, 128, 151
McKnight, William, 133
Machine organisation, *see* Organisations, machine
Meaning, xvii, 9, 28, 40, 60, 67, 71, 72, 82, 92, 94, 140, 166, 170
Measurement, 30, 114, 119
Merrill, Roger and Rebecca, 74
Microsoft, 129
Minimum critical specifications, 20
Mistakes, 27, 134
Mitroff, Ian, 1, 109
Model of Critical Leadership, xv, xvi
Moments of truth, 43, 44, 115, 145
Morale, 176
Morphogenesis, 4
Motivation, 57, 149, 150, 152, 157, 161
Motivation, *see* Performance
Mukhi, S., 188
Multiple realities, 110

National Training Council (NTC), 142
Nordstrom, 45, 143

Organisation, mind, 15
Organisational chart, 93–4
Organisational development, 33
Organisational structure, 8
Organisations, xvii, 13–38

Organisations, garden, 23, 29, 37–8, 103, 157, 169
Organisations, machine, xii, 23, 25, 28, 37–8, 86, 129, 130, 156, 157

Participative management, 91
Path–goal model, 186–8
Pay, 96
Peck, M. Scott, 39, 43, 46, 47, 54, 68, 132
People, xv, 8, 25, 98, 99, 152, 177
Performance, 61, 147, 148, 149, 151, 155, 156, 157, 165
Performance formula, 149, 156
Porras, Jerry I., 133
Posner, Barry Z., 62, 68, 120, 171
Prahalad, C. K., 23, 32, 54, 133, 144, 152
Preferred future, 13, 43, 46, 58, 59, 66, 80, 81, 100, 121, 122, 137, 141, 156
Probable future, 100
Purpose, 60, 61, 82, 84

Questioning, 121
Quick, Thomas, 108

Re-engineering, xi, 2, 13, 17, 32, 50, 53, 84
Recognition schemes, 42
Relationships, 1
Remuneration, 154, 168
Respect, 165
Restructuring, *see* Re-engineering
Results, 41
Retrenchments, 45
Revco, 21
Rewards, 95, 151
Richardson, Tony, 113
Ritz-Carlton, 81, 143
Roddick, Anita, 58, 172–3
Rules and regulations, 29, 95

203.

Index

Sacks, Oliver, 27
Schroedinger's Cat, 116
Scientific management, 91
Seeing, xvii, 1–12, 3, 4
Semler, Ricardo, 95
Senge, Peter, 102
Service quality, 145
Shareholders, 41
Sherrington, Sir Charles, 43
Simple, 92, 102
Singer, Edgar, 110
Situational theories, 178, 181–8
Six Thinking Hats, 135
Skinner, B. F., 151
Souffles, 116
Soul, 15
Strange attractors, 48
Structure, 8
Style theories, 178, 179–81
Subordinates, 8
Systems, 109, 177
Systems thinking, 91
Syzygy, 7, 8, 9, 10, 43, 46, 77, 78, 84, 149, 165
Sze, Arthur, 91

TARP, 143, 148
Taylor, Frederick, 95
Taylorism, 29, 75, 87
Theory X, 128, 151, 152, 153
Theory Y, 128, 151, 152, 153
Thinking hats, 135
Time, 70
Time management, 74
Training, 57

Trait theories, 178, 179
Transformation, xvii, 39, 49, 57, 39–59, 66, 68, 70, 70–1, 76, 80, 84, 86, 108, 109, 110, 113, 132 163
Truth, 117

Unbounded systems thinking (UST), 110
Unlearn, 133

Values, 68, 74–5, 78, 80, 82, 154, 165, 171
Vandermerwe, Sandra, 143
Virgil, 3, 4, 7
Vision, 74–5, 78, 80, 82
Vital Connections, xv, xvi, 9, 22, 42, 43, 45, 54, 56, 58, 70, 91, 98, 99, 105, 123, 125, 129, 130, 131, 132, 137, 140, 151, 158, 159, 160, 164, 165, 168
Volunteers, 39
Vroom, Victor H., 184–6

Wal-Mart, 135
Weisbord, Marvin, 54, 91, 99, 111, 141
Welch, Jack, 24, 30, 58, 59, 143
What it means to work here, 92, 94, 132, 167
Wheatley, Margaret, 14, 31, 77, 78, 85, 86, 117, 126
Womack, Cheryl, 145
Woodward, H., 66
Work descriptions, 97

Yetton, Philip, 184–6